paper books

Titles available in this series:

Martin Orkin

Shakespeare Against Apartheid

AD. DONKER / PUBLISHER

AD. DONKER (PTY) LTD
A subsidiary of Donker Holdings (Pty) Ltd
P.O. Box 41021
Craighall
2024

© Martin Orkin 1987

First published 1987

ISBN 0 86852 124 8

Typeset by Triangle Typesetters (Pty)Ltd, Johannesburg
Printed and bound by Creda Press (Pty) Ltd, Cape Town

To Joan
To Chloë
And To Mikhail

Contents

An early version of chapter 2 appeared as '*Hamlet* and the Security of the South African State' in *Contrast* 58, 15:2, 1984. 'Civility and the English Colonial Enterprise: Notes on Shakespeare's *Othello*', which appeared in *Literature in South Africa Today*, Special Issue of *Theoria*, 68, December 1986, and '*Othello* and the "plain face" of racism', which appears in *Shakespeare Quarterly*, 38:2, Summer 1987, are both partly based on chapter 3. 'Cruelty, *King Lear* and the South African Land Act 1913', partly based on chapter 4, appears in *Shakespeare Survey* 40. I should like to thank the editors and publishers of these journals for permission to use this material.

Foreword

This book attempts to suggest to undergraduate South African students, reading *Hamlet*, *Othello* and *King Lear* for the first time, points of departure for the study of the plays. I thought of writing it several years ago when I became aware, after teaching these works for a few years, of two major difficulties.

The first results from the fact that critics and teachers of Shakespeare in South Africa have tended and still tend to model their treatment of the text on traditional Anglo-American approaches, to which I refer briefly in chapter 1, 'Shakespeare Depoliticised'. The narrowness of this approach was worrying, although I did not then fully appreciate the crucial ways in which this was so. But even within the framework of traditional critical practice South African critics seemed to pay far less attention than their counterparts abroad to so many things — the detail of meaning in the lines, the poetry, the history from which the plays come. My primary reservation, however, was different. It related to the *effect* that this approach to the text had, and still has, within the South African situation. To make matters worse, those South African critics or teachers who then worked in Shakespeare studies (as many of them still do now) appeared to me uninterested in this effect and, equally, uninterested in moving beyond their approach. The emergence of new theories about literature developing Marxist, different structuralist, feminist, psychoanalytic or post-structuralist approaches, from the late sixties on, seemed also to be, by and large, ignored, certainly where the Shakespeare text was concerned, by those who had most influence in English departments in South Africa.

The second difficulty is that students in South African schools and those coming to university were, and still are, products of an educational system which works to legitimate the present South African social order. This system operates relentlessly by demonising all dissenting expression — political, social and economic — amongst other things by means of censorship, the banning of all political discussion and study in the school classroom and the rigid insistence on textbooks and syllabuses that either perpetuate the ideology of the dominant classes or contribute to their hegemony. Such a system not only deprives students of an awareness of alternatives, but their very capacity to analyse, or to envisage the enabling as well as the limiting possibilities in social, political and economic organisation, is also severely repressed.

In this situation, the particular treatment afforded certain 'great' literary texts serves to reinforce the dominant order's hegemony. Just as the text is said to have an intrinsic meaning independent of the world from which the work comes, pointing to certain abstract and idealised 'truths' (good and evil, honour and love, virtue and sin) about 'human nature', so the student is encouraged to believe that his/her identity is independent of social process and does not involve, for instance, the particular position he or she occupies in the established system of domination and subordination. The essential truths become *other-worldly* ones; the traditionalist approach reinforces in students the tendency to submission.

I have tried, in writing these introductions to *Hamlet, Othello* and *King Lear,* to take this consideration about undergraduates into account by attempting as far as possible to point a way forward beyond the traditionalist approach whilst not treating the kind of training which most students will have had in coming to the text as if it does not exist. For instance, in each chapter I have tried to identify that language in each play which points to levels of signification which traditional South African criticism was prepared to recognise. But at the same time, especially in the chapters on *Hamlet* and *Othello,* I have tried to indicate some elements in traditional Anglo-American approaches to the plays which the narrowness of South African criticism tended to ignore. Perhaps a little more deliberately in the chapters on *Othello* and *King Lear* I have tried to demonstrate not only the need to move towards identifiable theoretical approaches beyond the traditionalist one, but also to indicate those particular approaches which, in the South African context, appear to me especially at present, to be the most helpful and necessary.

I am now much more hopeful of the likelihood of escape from the traditional stranglehold on English Studies in South Africa where Shakespeare is concerned than I was when I first thought of writing this book. This is because of the immensely valuable work which has begun to appear in recent years, notably Stephen Greenblatt's *Renaissance Self-Fashioning* and *The Power of Forms in the English Renaissance* (edited by Greenblatt); Jonathan Dollimore's *Radical Tragedy;* Alan Sinfield's *Literature in Protestant England 1560—1660;* and Catherine Belsey's *Critical Practice.* Moreover, the recent publication of *Political Shakespeare* edited by Dollimore and Sinfield, and *Alternative Shakespeares* edited by John Drakakis will make a rapid and discernible difference. My deep indebtedness to these writers is evident throughout this book; its numerous defects of course remain my own. It seems to me that in the work of these critics and others like them, the future of Shakespeare studies in South Africa should especially lie. It is my hope that the present book, despite its many failings, will encourage students more quickly to take up these critical works and to choose from those theoretical paths which they suggest. In so doing we may read the Shakespeare text in ways that no longer subtly encourage a passive acceptance of the apartheid system but rather in ways that promote more active awareness of the possibility of alternatives to it.

I should like to record here my thanks and acknowledgements to a number of people. Firstly I owe whatever care I may have in the study of the Shakespeare text to the late Hilda M. Hulme whose example as scholar and teacher I can never hope to emulate but will always take as a source of inspiration. I should like also to thank Winifred Nowottny whose lectures and teaching on Shakespeare at University

College I shall never forget; in the *Othello* chapter I am particularly indebted to the lectures she gave on the play. I express my gratitude to a number of other people who, in one way or another, often through small words of advice or brief conversations the impact of which was, perhaps fortunately, unknown to them, or through more general actions of support, have helped me to complete this book: Michael Chapman, Stephen Clingman, Jonathan Dollimore, Noel Garson, Delayne Loppert, Max Loppert, Michael Mann, Barbara Mowat, Alan Sinfield, Alf Stadler, Charles van Onselen, Eddie Webster. Whatever value the following pages may have is due to this help; the faults, again, remain my own. I thank Lindsay Duncan for the care with which she went through the typescript. I would also like to thank my beloved parents Jenny and Morris Orkin for their continuing and always all-encompassing support. Chloë and Mikhail Orkin have restored my spirits when I most needed help. They, together with the unfailing conviction and support of my dear wife Joan Orkin, the necessary condition, have made the writing of this book possible.

1 Shakespeare Depoliticised

'Reade him, therefore; and againe, and againe,' wrote Heminge and Condell, Shakespeare's first editors in 1623, 'and if then you doe not like him, surely you are in some manifest danger, not to understand him,' but their advice begs questions that have recently been most excitingly addressed in Shakespeare studies.[1] These questions consider not only issues such as who is doing the reading, but also the conditions determining the production of the work, for whom it was produced and so on. They provide evidence of the great strides in the development of new theoretical approaches to the study of literature taken in the last twenty years or so, which have moved decisively away from traditional approaches — often based upon various kinds of New Criticism — which tended to be dominant in university English Departments. At the same time though, such questions themselves relate to the context of their own production, confirming the truism that every age understands Shakespeare in its own way. We cannot escape our own mode of seeing or, some would have it, our own particular discourse. Perhaps this is still partly the work of that old-fashioned protagonist, time. Johnson, who wrote in not only a pre-structuralist age but also a pre-post-structuralist age, saw it like that when he wondered about some of what were to him Shakespeare's obscurities. These could only alert him, he said, to the existence of meanings now 'lost with the objects to which they were united, as the figures vanish when the canvas has decayed.'[2]

In this comment we may detect a hint of recognition that the work of art comes from a particular context and that understanding that work involves responding to it as an element within the larger canvas of its own time. That larger context and the individual works of art that come from it we may only appreciate through study of available work about or from the Elizabethan and Jacobean world, together with

study of the Shakespeare text. But there is the other problem. Even though we may have access to written material
we remain located in our own world and the way in which
we read will be significantly determined by this fact. The
work has its place at one particular historical moment and
we who study it occupy our place at another. The multiplicity of readings of Shakespeare that have occurred, since
he wrote, in succeeding ages partly bears witness to the extent to which the product of one moment can be perceived
only by means of rather than despite the discourses available
at another.

The indeterminacy of readings, for this and other reasons,
has loomed large as an issue in recent critical writing. We do
need to respond to the text but the way in which we do this,
some would say the way in which we appropriate it, will always be a vital issue. And in South Africa, the attempt to
read Shakespeare's plays, even in the last decades of the
twentieth century, presents its own special difficulties.

Until fairly recently the 'traditional' approach to the
tragedies in South Africa involved a more or less exclusive
focus upon the hero in the plays, the identification of certain
moral truths about 'human nature' and, as the plays unfold,
recognition of an 'order' or 'harmony' which, despite possible
breakdown, manifests recovery through 'insight' and the defeat of 'evil'. Thus, in an issue of *English Studies in Africa*
devoted exclusively to Shakespeare, and published in 1977,
one article on *King Lear*, attempting to explore Shakespeare's
comic themes and strategies, suggests that the play, in the
first four acts, finds its pattern in the archetype of the mad
Nebuchadnezzar who has pride, who falls and is put into
exile, 'which accords with the paradigm of the Fall of Man
and his conversion and redemption in Christ', a pattern con-
cluded with the recognition of his sin.[3] When it moves beyond detailed concerns to refer to the play as a whole this
article identifies only a process of 'distortion by sin' (p.30),
'the deforming power of sin' (p. 31), or the 'transforming
power of sin' (p. 36). Another article, in the same number,
concerned with *Hamlet*, occupies itself exclusively with a
detailed discussion of the issue of delay in the character

Hamlet.[4] The article on *Othello,* starting with the observation: 'as with all other important figures in Shakespeare's tragedies, Othello's individuality is most elaborately and subtly delineated; and the subtleties of his character have been analysed by many critics — and perhaps most notably by Bradley,'[5] but disclaiming a concern with character as such, claims that the play offers a 'demonstration of one of the frightening possibilities about love' (p. 15). Nevertheless it finds that the plot is 'the means whereby in the *protagonist'* (my emphasis) such possibilities are turned into actuality and that

for Shakespeare, as for any literary artist, the story is clearly partly an artifice — not a realistic account of the way human events would be likely to turn out in everyday life, but a convincing image of the way things *might essentially be*: an image created in the process of distilling an insight into, or a revelation of, human nature (p. 15).

This article concludes by arguing that we must react to the end of *Othello* with its 'loss of harmony' and 'balance' with 'recognition, wonder, fear and awe. . . we must learn all that we can from tragic events, we must love and admire all that is generous in thought, in feeling and in deed; but above all or beneath all we must be humble' (p. 24).

The conclusion in this final sentence strikingly suggests the use to which Shakespeare has been put in encouraging particular attitudes — a longing for instruction in certain abstractions about human behaviour, a pseudo-fatalistic or stoic resignation about the frailties of this world, acceptance of the status quo. Of the many other responses that might be offered to the approach manifest in these articles, however, I should like to provide only one here. It attends not so much to the nature of what the articles offer as to what they *avoid.* None of them considers, to any noteworthy degree, aspects of the socio-political world evident within the plays, within which the characters with whom they are so engaged, are located. Nor do they consider to any worthwhile extent that context from which the play comes. Their common approach is of course influenced, as the one quotation supplied above indicates, primarily by Bradley — each article makes a point of mentioning Bradley in one way or another — relying on Bradley's assertion that the centre of tragedy lies in 'action issuing from character, or in character issuing in action.'[6]

South African critics continued to indulge in this avoidance during the sixties and seventies despite the fact that Shakespearean criticism in England and America was never so narrow. David Bevington, in his book *Tudor Politics and the Drama*, published in 1968, for instance, described 'a pattern of many sided debate in political dramaturgy' and demonstrated that by the turn of the sixteenth century the English were quite used to the presentation of political issues on stage:

To the dispassionate theatre goer around the year 1600 it must have seemed as though the English Reformation, and the long years of Elizabeth's reign, had settled nothing. Discussions of royal succession, obedience to authority, the efficacy of public justice, and the dangers of religious civil war were central to most plays one could see, public or private.[7]

One of the most distinguished Shakespeare scholars of the twentieth century, Kenneth Muir, recognised four years earlier than this not only the political thrust in Shakespeare's plays but identified also an ambiguity in their handling of political issues:

He [Shakespeare] had read, like everyone else, the propaganda on behalf of the Tudor settlement, but we do not know how far he accepted it. His plays could not be performed without a licence; and on one occasion when Shakespeare tried to satisfy the censorship by rewriting the riot scenes in *Sir Thomas More*, the ban was not lifted. His patron, the Earl of Southampton, was one of the Essex conspirators; and, on the eve of their fatuous insurrection, Shakespeare's company was persuaded to give a subsidised performance of *Richard II* because the play showed the deposing of a king. The actors got into serious trouble, in spite of the very orthodox views on rebellion expressed in the play. It is the only play, indeed, in which the theory of the Divine Right of Kings is expounded or assumed by sympathetic characters. In *Hamlet* the doctrine is put into the mouths of Rosencrantz and Guildenstern in support of the murdering usurper Claudius.[8]

The bias in traditional South African criticism of the Shakespeare text — its preference for emphasis upon individual rather than socio-political concerns in the plays — coincides in its effects with that bias deliberately aimed at by the educative philosophy propounded by the dominant classes. Its emphasis effectively depoliticises as well as misrecognises certain possibilities that may be found in the Shakespeare text.[9] It is perhaps not surprising that South African critics often so doggedly stick to their Bradley, a late Victorian scholar who worked within an educative system that served the interests of an imperial English ruling class which believed itself (with of course the right kind of character building at public school and university) free to determine its fate.[10] True, the function of traditional literary criticism in general in South Africa has been much discussed in recent years and need not be attended to here.[11] But somehow in such discussions, Shakespeare has been mostly left alone in his 'traditional' guise, presumably to represent and bolster what is also regarded as a dying breed.

Certainly the narrow traditional South African approach to Shakespeare must be destined, like Pope's prude, to the gnome's embrace — let us hope sooner rather than later. But it has regrettably helped to bring the Shakespeare text itself, for the moment, into disrepute. The plays together with works by other writers have been bitingly dismissed as instruments of hegemony. Discussing the need for new techniques of writing, Mothobi Mutloatse argues, 'we will have to *donder* conventional literature: old fashioned critic and reader alike. . . we are going to pee and spit and shit on literary convention before we are through.'[12]

In the American and English critical world, if traditional criticism was never so narrow as that in South Africa, the sixties and seventies brought also the outburst and growth of new approaches so that such a response to the Shakespeare text was never likely. On the contrary, materialist criticism, especially, developed exploration of the ways in which texts *reveal* the extent to which individuals are significantly shaped and determined by the processes in which they are placed. Or, again, it explored ways in which texts themselves both reflect and also respond to the existing relations of domination and subordination within which they occur.

Such approaches to Shakespeare may occasionally, in turn, prompt reference to the particular conditions within which audience or reader may be located. Moreover, modern practitioners in theatre have not been slow to demonstrate this. Earlier in the twentieth century both Artaud and Brecht, in developing their own engagement with drama, found inspiration from Jacobean theatre. More recently, the English dramatist Edward Bond, located in a twentieth-century industrialised state recognises the extent to which a play coming from a late feudal and early capitalist pre-industrialised world, in the very way in which it relates to the particulars of its context, prompts in him an awareness of the parallels in his own contemporary experience. Describing his visit, in a school party, to a performance of *Macbeth,* Edward Bond recalls: 'For the first time in my life, I met somebody who was actually talking about my problems about the life I'd been living, the political society around me.'[13] Again, the materialist critic Robert Weimann, in the sixties, observed that 'the universalizing pattern in Shakespeare and the "myriad-mindedness" of his art were never outside history' but he also went on to note that the plays 'live beyond the historical conditions that made them possible. . . It was because Shakespeare and his theatre were so much the "Soule of the Age" that his work continues to live, as it were, "for all time".'[14]

The Shakespeare text primarily has interest in terms of its relationship to the world from which it comes but it must be recognised that in South Africa, the extent to which we may be prepared to react to certain issues in the text, such as those relating to power, injustice and political or social exploitation and oppression, will depend upon more than attention to the text itself and debate about its context. It may depend too upon the extent to which we in our own world are aware of and ready to recognise related issues. Such a prerequisite may well have been understood by the critics in South Africa who chose and often still choose to stick to 'traditional' emphases, to dwell upon the abstract eternal 'truth' rather than upon the particular reality. And in resisting this tendency in criticism it may be necessary for us to *start* with awareness of ourselves, situated as we are in a semi-industrialised, capitalist, *apartheid* state, during a period of crisis and collapse, that may also be one of transition, a period that, as has been the case especially in the last fifty or so years, is still characterised by brutal exploitation and repression. In this way we may be more equipped to identify certain concerns in a text that itself comes from a totally different context, but one also characterised by transition and great change in the social order. As Dollimore and Sinfield point out: 'The Elizabethan state was in transition from a feudal to a bourgeois structure, and this had entailed and was to entail considerable violent disruption.'[15] Theatre in this world was complex:

On the one hand, it was sometimes summoned to perform at Court and as such may seem a direct extension of royal power. . . on the other hand, it was the mode of cultural production in which market forces were strongest, and as such it was especially exposed to the influence of subordinate. . . classes (p. 211).

In studying these plays, Dollimore and Sinfield argue that we should expect always to find evidence of this complexity: 'We should not. . . expect any straightforward relationship between plays and ideology: on the contrary, it is even likely that topics which engaged writers and audiences alike were those where ideology was under strain' (p. 211).

To recognise issues such as those relating to power and justice with which Shakespeare seems in certain plays to be crucially engaged at his own moment in history, as Weimann seems to recommend, and to register awareness, as Bond does, of related issues present at our own point in time is never to suggest that the two moments lose their particularity, can ever be the *same*. But those issues, different as they are, may nevertheless speak to aspects of our world. And despite the dominant influence of traditional critics in past decades there were a few dissenting voices within South Africa perceiving this. In 1965 Lewis Nkosi recalled the vibrancy of the Shakespeare text for some of the people living in the Sophiatown of the fifties:

Ultimately, it was the cacophonous, swaggering world of Elizabethan England which gave us the closest parallel to our own mode of existence; the cloak and dagger stories of Shakespeare; the marvellously gay and dangerous time of change in Great Britain, came closest to reflecting our own condition. Thus it was possible for an African musician returning home at night to inspire awe in a group of thugs surrounding him by declaiming in an impossibly archaic English: 'Unhand me, rogues!' Indeed, they did unhand him. The same thugs who were to be seen chewing on apples in the streets of Johannesburg after the manner of the gangsters they had seen in Richard Widmark's motion picture, *Street with no Name,* also delighted in the violent colour, the rolling rhetoric of Shakespearean theatre. Their favourite form of persecuting middle-class Africans was forcing them to stand at street corners, reciting some passage from Shakespeare, for which they would be showered with sincere applause.[16]

This book offers a brief introduction to *Hamlet, Othello* and *King Lear,* three of Shakespeare's plays which raise issues of particular interest to a South African audience. It attempts to argue that we should, when we study Shakespeare, more readily and extensively acknowledge who, as well as where, we are. Therefore, when we examine the text and when we also examine historical discourse, we should be ready to notice those moments of parallel that may prove fruitful both for our reading of the play and for our awareness of our own particular context. The extent to which we attempt to do these things may be the extent to which we cease to depoliticise and misrecognise the Shakespeare text and begin, instead, to treat it in a less disabled way — in the way his first editors, in a manner of speaking, enjoined.

Notes

1 C. Hinman ed., *The First Folio of Shakespeare,* The Norton Facsimile (New York: W.W. Norton and Co., 1968), p. 7. (some spelling modernised).

2 Samuel Johnson, 'Proposals for Printing by Subscription The Dramatic Works of William Shakespeare', in *The Yale Edition of the Works of Samuel Johnson*, vol. VII, ed. Arthur Sherbo (New Haven: Yale University Press, 1968), p. 53.

3 Peter Bryant, 'Nuncle Lear', *English Studies in Africa*, 20:1, 1977, pp. 27—41, p. 28.

4 G.F. Hartford, 'Once More Delay', *English Studies in Africa* 20:1, 1977, pp. 1—9.

5 C.O. Gardner, 'Tragic Fission in *Othello*', *English Studies in Africa* 20:1, 1977, pp. 11—25, p. 14.

6 A.C. Bradley, *Shakespearean Tragedy* (London: Macmillan, 1961), p. 7. John Drakakis ed., *Alternative Shakespeares* (London: Methuen, 1985), pp. 1—25, gives a useful account of Bradley's views and the tradition in which he participates. See also Katherine Cooke, *A.C. Bradley and his influence in Twentieth Century Shakespeare Criticism* (Oxford: Oxford University Press, 1972).

7 David Bevington, *Tudor Drama and Politics* (Cambridge, Massachusetts: Harvard University Press, 1968), p. 298, p. 290.

8 Kenneth Muir, 'Shakespeare and Politics' in *Shakespeare in a Changing World*, ed. Arnold Kettle (Wellingborough: Lawrence & Wishart, 1964), p. 66.

9 Jonathan Dollimore and Alan Sinfield, 'History and Ideology: the instance of *Henry V*' in Drakakis, *Alternative Shakespeares*, p. 212, write of the tendency to represent the social order as 'immutable and unalterable', 'decreed by God or simply natural'. 'One religious vision represented ultimate reality in terms of unity and stasis: human endeavour, governed by the laws of change and occupying the material domain, is ever thwarted in its aspiration, ever haunted by its loss of an absolute which can only be regained in transcendance. . . This metaphysical vision has its political uses, especially when aiding the process of subjection by encouraging renunciation of the material world and a disregard of its social aspects such that oppression is experienced as a fate rather than an "alterable condition".'

10 Dollimore and Sinfield, 'History and Ideology: the instance of *Henry V*', p. 212, writing of the sixteenth and seventeenth centuries note the Protestant doctrine of callings. Perkins writes 'God bestows his gifts upon us. . . that they might be employed in his service and to his glory and that in his life' — which Sinfield discusses more fully in *Literature in Protestant England 1560—1660* (London: Croom Helm, 1983). Dollimore and Sinfield continue: 'This doctrine legitimated the expansive assertiveness of a social order which was bringing much of Britain under centralised con-

21

trol, colonising parts of the New World and trading vigorously with most of the Old, and which was to experience revolutionary changes. At the same time acquiescence in an unjust social order (like that encouraged by a fatalistic metaphysics of stasis) seemed to be effected, though less securely, by an insistence that "whatsoever any man enterpriseth or doth, either in word or deed, he must do it by virtue of his calling, and he must keep himself within the compass, limits, or precincts thereof".'

11 See *Critical Arts: A Journal for Media Studies*, 3:2, 1984. The whole volume is devoted to the theme 'English Studies in Transition'.

12 Mothobi Mutloatse ed., *Forced Landing* (Johannesburg: Ravan, 1980) Editor's introduction, p. 5.

13 Edward Bond quoted in the introduction, p. v, (from interview with editors of *Theatre Quarterly*, 11:5, Jan — Mar 1972) to *Lear*, ed. Patricia Hern (London: Methuen, 1983).

14 Robert Weimann, 'The Soul of the Age: Towards a Historical Approach to Shakespeare' in *Shakespeare in a Changing World*, ed. Arnold Kettle, p. 42.

15 Dollimore and Sinfield, 'History and Ideology: the instance of *Henry V*', p. 219.

16 Lewis Nkosi, 'The Fabulous Decade: the fifties' in *Home and Exile* (USA: Longmans, 1983), p. 13.

2 *Hamlet* and the Security of the South African State

The true nature of the state power portrayed in *Hamlet* declares itself in Act IV when Claudius, knowing that Hamlet is aware of his secret murder of the previous ruler of Denmark, announces that he has decided to send the young prince to England. Then, left alone on stage, he confirms that he intends to eliminate his opponent:

> And England, if my love thou hold'st at aught —
> As my great power thereof may give thee sense,
> Since yet thy cicatrice looks raw and red
> After the Danish sword, and thy free awe
> Pays homage to us — thou mayst not coldly set
> Our sovereign process, which imports at full,
> By letters congruing to that effect,
> The present death of Hamlet. Do it, England;
> For like the hectic in my blood he rages,
> And thou must cure me.
>
> (IV. iii. 70)[1]

Claudius's intention to have Hamlet murdered — although he does not succeed in the play — and the duplicity with which he proceeds confirm him as a practitioner of violence, recalcitrant and ruthless when it comes to the preservation of his own power. The text also identifies the inter-relatedness of such a ruler and his society directly when Rosencrantz, unaware of the ironies of what he is saying, observes elsewhere in the play to the King himself:

> The cess of majesty
> Dies not alone, but like a gulf doth draw
> What's near it with it. Or it is a massy wheel
> Fix'd on the summit of the highest mount,

23

To whose huge spokes ten thousand lesser things
Are mortis'd and adjoin'd, which when it falls,
Each small annexment, petty consequence,
Attends the boist'rous ruin. Never alone
Did the King sigh, but with a general groan.

(III. iii. 23)

This recognition of the inter-relatedness of ruler and ruled reflected a well-known Elizabethan notion. A similar identification which registers the magnitude of impact of the dominant class not only in its retaliation against those who threaten aspects of, or oppose, the existing social order but also in its domination of those who submit to it emerges from an account in present day South Africa of a recent tragic event, representative of many other similar cases. The 1981 Race Relations Survey contains the following report relating to the death of Steve Biko:

A committee appointed by the Medical Association of South Africa (MASA) to investigate the medical ethical issues arising from the conduct of two doctors involved in the treatment of Black Consciousness leader Mr Steve Biko shortly before his death, published its report in August. Mr Biko died in detention on September 14, [sic] 1978, after being detained on August 18, and widespread criticism of Drs Ivor Lang and Benjamin Tucker followed the inquest into his death. The committee, consisting of Mr I.A. Maisels, QC and Dr J.N. de Villiers, found that:

—   it was undesirable that the security police headquarters in Pretoria should have the power to decide whether or not a detainee should be removed to a non-prison hospital;
—   medical practitioners should directly ask detainees themselves what their health problems were;
—   the medical profession should not allow a doctor to absolve himself of responsibility if his medical advice was rejected by security police headquarters;
—   in the event of being overruled by the security police, the doctor should report this to the Minister of Police and try to obtain the support of his local medical association.

Because it did not have any subpoena powers, the committee did not attempt to establish whether the doctors involved were guilty of disgraceful or unprofessional conduct. However, the committee did find

that a medical certificate issued by Dr Lang, presently the Port Elizabeth District Surgeon, concerning Mr Biko's condition shortly before
his death was 'unsatisfactory and incomplete, if not a deliberate sup-
pression of the facts'.

In the certificates he drew up, Dr Lang said he could not establish
the existence of any abnormality affecting Mr Biko's health, even
though Mr Biko was behaving strangely and would not speak. The committee also found that Colonel P.J. Goosen, the security policeman in
charge of Mr Biko's detention, regarded himself and the security police
as being above the law. Dr Lang and Dr Tucker were forbidden by the
Deputy Director of Health Services, Dr D.J. Gillilland, from participa-
ting in the committee's proceedings. The committee was refused permission to inspect the Walmer Police Station cells where Mr Biko was
held.[2]

This report does not simply involve the mysterious death of a
political detainee whilst in the custody of state power. It
mentions a number of individuals directly involved in or subsequently drawn into the incidents described. Moreover it
raises disturbing questions of responsibility involving support
for, acquiescence in or opposition to the actions of the dominant order. And it underlines the extent to which individuals
within the state are in one way or another implicated in political events of terrible magnitude.

The presentation of a ruler such as Claudius in *Hamlet*
should not surprise us. Relationships between the dominant
and subordinate orders and between different interest groups
within the dominant order in the Elizabethan state were
problematic. Apart from anything else, although Elizabeth
towards the end of her reign remained the accepted monarch,
this was not a simple matter. For one thing the ruling class
continued to encounter, coerce and persecute dissent or
opposition; to do this it was never averse to the use of
methods of government we now term totalitarian: censorship, spies, unlimited power of arrest, detention, torture and
execution. B.L. Joseph describes the treatment of Puritans,
for instance, in the last two decades of the sixteenth century:

Between the end of 1587 and ... 1589 Puritan opposition to the Crown
showed itself in the Marprelate pamphlets, but eventually the anony-
mous authors had to stop to avoid discovery. One of the chief writers,

John Penry, escaped to Scotland, but was lured back and executed in 1593 . . . The government treated extreme Puritans as if they were Anabaptists, dedicated in the imaginations of the ruling circles and of the populace to the subversion of church, state and public morals. In 1589 a group of Presbyterian leaders, including Cartwright, were summoned by the commission, refused to take the oath and were sent to prison until 1592, when they were released because no open infringement of the law could be proved against them. But the more extreme Puritans suffered much more. John Udall, suspected of being a Martinist, was sentenced to death but died in prison before execution in 1590. One, Hackett, accused of plotting against the Queen's life, was executed in 1592. In 1593, Barrow and Greenwood, the separatists, were executed for seditious speeches . . . [3]

Such governmental methods were obviously not applied only in the case of Puritan opponents. And if Elizabeth herself was never perceived to be a tyrant by the majority of her subjects, religious issues throughout Europe made the problem of a tyrannous ruler highly topical. The English uncertainty about a future without Elizabeth only intensified the topicality of this subject. Yet interestingly it was a modern East European critic, amongst others, who was to encourage attention to the importance of the political concerns in *Hamlet*. Praising a production of the play which he saw in Poland, Jan Kott wrote in 1965:

The *Hamlet* produced in Cracow a few weeks after the XXth Congress of the Soviet Communist Party lasted exactly three hours. It was light and clear, tense and sharp, modern and consistent. . . It was a political drama *par excellence*. 'Something is rotten in the state of Denmark' — was the first chord of *Hamlet's* new meaning. And then the dead sound of the words 'Denmark's a prison', three times repeated. Finally the magnificent churchyard scene, with the gravediggers' dialogue rid of metaphysics, brutal and unequivocal. Gravediggers know for whom they dig graves. 'The gallows is built stronger than the church' they say.[4]

Within the Elizabethan dominant classes too, there was considerable conflict of interest. For many reasons, some of which the chapter on *King Lear* will enumerate, Elizabeth's position

as monarch was far from absolute. She could maintain her
position only through a combination of

political adroitness, patronage and force — and all these, the latter
especially, could be exercised only by and through the aristocracy itself.
Elizabeth could oppose the Earl of Leicester if supported by Burghley,
or vice versa, but she could not for long oppose them both. After the
death of Leicester in 1589 the power struggle was not so symmetrical.
The rise of the youthful, charismatic and militarily impressive Earl of
Essex introduced a new element: he rivalled the Queen herself, as
Burghley and Leicester never did. The more service, especially military, Essex performed, the more he established a rival power base, and
Elizabeth did not care for it. . . The Irish expedition was make or break
for both; Essex would be away from court and vulnerable to schemes
against him, but were he to return with spectacular success he would be
unstoppable. In the event he was not successful, and thus found himself
pushed into a corner where he could see no alternative but direct revolt.[5]

David Bevington makes a strong case against topical identification in the plays of historical personages and events.[6] But
there is no need to suggest that Hamlet is Essex to recognise
the significance, in 1601, of a play presenting conflict within
the ruling class. Furthermore Essex's hopes for the succession
centred round James of Scotland, but great uncertainty sur-
rounded the prospect of such a ruler ascending the English
throne. If Elizabeth herself was never perceived to be a tyrant
by the majority of her subjects the religious question made
tyrannous action in a ruler the issue for all dissenters in every
country in Europe, including, as we have just seen, those
dissenting in matters of religion in England. The fact that
James was untested and also, in his religious sympathies, suspected, might in 1601 have encouraged the exploration on
stage of issues involving opposition to a tyrannous ruler.
    Such antagonisms, divisions and uncertainties within the
dominant order, as well as religious and other forms of
dissent, to say nothing of the economic and social flux of the
period, were for obvious reasons resisted in the propositions
of Elizabethan state ideology. These worked to legitimate
the existing social order and to present it as unified, naturally

hierarchical and ultimately sanctioned by God. Rosencrantz's flattery of Claudius in Act III, scene iii, lines 15—23 not only recognises the inter-relatedness of ruler and ruled but also presupposes the principle of hierarchy. Claudius himself relies on this proposition when he is confronted by a potentially rebellious Laertes:

> Do not fear our person.
> There's such divinity doth hedge a king
> That treason can but peep to what it would,
> Acts little of his will
>
> (IV. v. 125)

Claudius knows that he can count on the ignorance of the court and its support of the 'official' view of monarchy; indeed, the first word that is uttered when he is finally killed is 'treason' (V. ii. 328). But the contradictions in such a claim set against the man who utters it are evident. That such an attitude to monarchy was deliberately promoted by the ruling class might never have seemed a more inviting inference, held in check perhaps, by the rider that the speaker is a usurper and a tyrant. This strategy of legitimation, as we in the twentieth century may readily recognise, often goes hand in hand with the misrepresentation of opposition or dissent as treachery. The claim of 'treason' appears to be purely a function of the partisan views of the accusers. In the famous treason trials of the late fifties in South Africa, many individuals were brought to a lengthy and disruptive trial, only to be acquitted at the end of it all. Soon after this, detention without trial was introduced, enabling the minister, at his own discretion, to decide who was a danger to the state. Nor did this present any problem of conscience for the man who introduced these laws. When asked, 'Are you saying that if the government of the day identifies a man as a threat to the State then it is its duty to lock that man up, even without the benefit of a trial?' he was happy to reply, 'If I see a man or a woman as a threat to the State and if there are valid reasons for not bringing that person to trial, then I must take them out of circulation one way or another. That is my responsibility as Minister of Justice.'[7]

2

The moral issues precipitating Hamlet's dilemma about revenge have been described by many critics.[8] The ghost asks of the prince adherence to the code of family honour, thrusting against this, Christianity forbids murderous action, warning that God alone is the only judge. Before the end of the play-scene, moreover, Hamlet's problems are exacerbated by the uncertain origins of the ghost.[9] To this we need to add the fact that legitimation (with the help of the doctrines of hierarchy and the Divine Right of Kings), of the ruling class's position within the social order also occurred in a context of lively debate about the right of resistance to rulers. Roland Mushat Frye, who in some respects follows a traditional approach to *Hamlet,* has demonstrated at length that in Shakespeare's day a variety of attitudes on the subject were current.[10]

The official Tudor view forbade resistance to the ruling monarch, however questionable his rights to the throne, a perspective, which Frye claims, many Englishmen shared. Thus *The Book of Homilies,* appointed to be read in churches, commands obedience and condemns wilful rebellion.[11] But Frye argues that even among those who held the official Anglican doctrine of non-resistance to the crown, cases of conscience involving obedience and disobedience were not always easy to resolve.[12] He cites as one example of this, Bishop Hooper's support of Princess Mary, despite the fact that, with the support of Archbishop Cranmer, the virtually unanimous support of the judges of the realm and the unanimous acceptance of the royal council, Lady Jane Grey had already been proclaimed the new monarch, on the death of King Edward VI. Shortly before his execution as a heretic in 1555, Hooper, defending himself, recalled his support of Mary despite the fact that the council had already 'freely gone along' with Lady Jane Gray:

As for my truth and loyalty to the Queen's highness, the time of her most dangerous estate can testify with me, that when there was both commandments and commissions out against her, whereby she was, to the sight of the world, the more in danger, and less like to come to the crown; yet, when she was at the worst, I rode myself from place to place. . . to win and stay the people for her party: and whereas another was proclaimed [Jane Grey], I preferred her [Mary] notwithstanding the proclamations.[13]

And during Edward VI's reign Hooper had preached a sermon which reasoned that the process of coronation itself did not make the king, but only the right of succession.[14]

Another view of resistance attempted to define it in the context of retribution or retaliation. Tyndale argued that Christ's absolute commandment against vengeance applied to the private citizen only, not to the ruler or magistrate, who is not disabled from administering justice, thus developing a long established distinction between private person and official ruler: 'Christ here intended not to disannul the temporal regiment, and to forbid rulers to punish evil doers. . . [the ruler] not only mayest, but also must, and art bound under pain of damnation to execute [his] office.'[15]

Frye recalls in this context the notorious murder of James I's father, Lord Darnley, who, after he was married to Mary Queen of Scots, was referred to as 'King Henry'. His murdered body was found in an orchard and his most likely assassin, the Earl of Bothwell married the widowed queen and moved toward the crown. James's paternal grandparents laid the challenge of revenge squarely upon their infant grandson in a memorial painting the details of which actively enjoined on him the task of exacting retribution.[16]

Finally, Frye points out that European Catholics and Protestants in certain instances argued that resistance was a necessity:

The Protestant monarchomachs. . . [attempted] to establish inclusive justifications for overthrowing a tyrant. Even though he might not be a usurper, a ruler who 'violates the bonds and shatters the restraints by which human society has been maintained,' as Althusius put it, would in this view leave magnates and princes of the blood no other recourse than to take up arms. In striking down a tyrant, according to Buchanan, they would be engaged in 'the most just of wars'. Not only did princes and magistrates have the right to destroy a tyrant, but they had the duty to do so, according to teachings shared by Calvinists and Jesuits. As the Huguenot du Plessis-Mornay put it, they are not only permitted 'to use force against a tyrant. . . but obliged as part of the duty of their office, and they have no excuse if they should fail to act'. In a somewhat more general context, Calvin wrote of inactive magistrates that if they 'put up their sword and hold their hands pure from blood while in the meantime desperate men do reign with murders and slaughters, then they shall make themselves guilty of most great wickedness.'[17]

Ideological legitimation stressing hierarchy and order occurred, in the context then, of a range of views regarding resistance to a usurper or tyrant who was also the crowned monarch. Moreover attempts on the ruler's life happened in the sixteenth and seventeenth centuries both in England and in Europe; two of these, against Henry III of France in 1589 and against Henry IV of France in 1610, were successful.

If the issues in Hamlet's situation are, in these ways, highly suggestive, the fact that the prince spends the first four acts debating them places him in considerable political danger. From the official point of view to avenge his father means also to rid his class of its established ruler. Were his movement into a position of contestation with this ruler made public he would be classifiable as the equivalent of what some twentieth century governments mean by an 'enemy' of the state. His first concern therefore is to ensure absolute secrecy — he realises he will have to 'go underground'. After the departure of the Ghost he urges his friends to swear that they will never reveal what has transpired — in seventeenth-century Christian terms his insistence upon an oath has obvious importance. Furthermore, envisaging what measures of self-protection will in future have to be adopted, he tries to prevent discovery by a watchful and suspicious ruler:

> But come,
> Here, as before, never, so help you mercy,
> How strange or odd some'er I bear myself —
> As I perchance hereafter shall think meet
> To put an antic disposition on —
> That you, at such time seeing me, never shall,
> With arms encumber'd thus, or this head-shake,

31

Or by pronouncing of some doubtful phrase,
As 'Well, we know', or 'We could and if we would',
Or 'If we list to speak', or 'There be and if they might',
Or such ambiguous giving out, to note
That you know aught of me — this do swear,
So grace and mercy at your most need help you.

(I. v. 188)

Shakespeare took the device of madness from his sources, but used it in more than one way. Hamlet's subsequent 'antic disposition' may in part be an emblem of torment, or a means of communicating his satire about the tendency to compromise with and accept the prevailing behaviour of the dominant order. It is as well a mask, adapted as a political tactic to hide as best he can the truth of his antagonism towards the established ruler. Furthermore, in a social order where behaviour is never free of the surveillance of agents of the ruling class Hamlet understands that every move of his associates will be scrutinised for their political implications. The young prince of Denmark is well aware of the political difficulties arising from the demand which the ghost of his father has made.

3

Hamlet's understanding of the political implications of what the Ghost has asked him to do, and his awareness of the alertly watchful and potentially treacherous nature of members of the court make him tread warily, but he must do so also because Claudius is a formidable opponent.

If the King has the doctrine of the Divine Right of Kings and absolute power as a means of self-protection the text also presents Claudius, as many critics observe, as a ruler with a great deal of political acumen.[18] His opening speech to the court, despite its ironies, displays great skill in reconciling the old dispensation with the new and in using the possibility of foreign threat as a rallying point; in the course of the play, he resolves the crisis with Norway without war and without compromising the rights of Denmark.

Claudius's political adroitness is also revealed in his ability to exploit the unsuspecting loyalty of his subjects. In the name of legitimate rule he involves them in duplicity; in fact he uses those prepared to work for him to hunt out and if possible destroy any threat to the retention at all costs of his own power.

In the dealings which the King has with Polonius and with Rosencrantz and Guildenstern, the text demonstrates Cladius's skill in exploiting the loyalty of his subjects whilst at the same time illustrating the nature of those prepared to compromise their own actions in the names of their rulers. There is one moment when Polonius, compromising Ophelia too in the business of spying upon Hamlet, recognises the betrayal of honesty and straight dealing which his readiness to spy for the King involves.

> Read on this book,
> That show of such an exercise may colour
> Your loneliness. — We are oft to blame in this,
> 'Tis too much prov'd, that with devotion's visage
> The devil himself
>
> (III. i. 49)

Polonius is never aware of the real motive for Claudius's concern about Hamlet, nor does he understand the nature of Claudius's kingship. In him *Hamlet* presents to us the man who operates within the dominant order unquestioningly. Our first real glimpse of the councillor occurs in Act I scene iii when we see him giving advice to both his children. The precepts he offers to Laertes were well known, often memorised by children who attended grammar schools.[19] Shakespeare's first audiences would recognise in Polonius's predilection for such commonplace expressions of worldly wisdom a mind that runs along conventional tracks, sticking only to what is practically useful in terms of worldly self-advancement. His advice to Laertes, as with his advice to Ophelia, focuses on social survival and success within the dominant order. Thus when he speaks to Ophelia about Hamlet he sees her relationship with the prince exclusively in expedient social terms. He may of course be entitled to point out to his daughter the 'political realities' that might make any real relationship with Hamlet difficult, but he does not for a moment credit either Ophelia or Hamlet with any capacity for mutual love and respect.

He describes Hamlet's behaviour as that of a worldly exploiter, setting 'springes to catch woodcocks' (I. iii. 115), and he sees love in the language of financial broking or later, in the context of his son's activities in Paris, in the language of promiscuity.[20] This failure of Polonius's mind and imagination to go beyond the mundane, more cynical worldly view of experience is evident too when Hamlet discusses theatre. Polonius's consciousness appreciates neither the value of theatre nor the richness of Hamlet's response to it. It is precisely because he tends to the well worn path, eschewing or pouring scorn on the exceptional in human experience that Polonius becomes so useful a tool to a ruler like Claudius. His readiness to accept, compromise, follow the empirical and expedient path becomes a readiness to accept that the end justifies the means, as he himself admits, that to catch the 'carp of truth' the 'bait of falsehood' (II. i. 63) is necessary:

> thus do we of wisdom and of reach,
> With windlasses and with assays of bias,
> By indirections find directions out.
>   (II. i. 66)

Not himself a man of conscious malice he is not a man of principle either, and in this he is exactly like Rosencrantz and Guildenstern. Young as they are they hold a similar pragmatic and expedient political attitude. They are ready to return to Denmark at the summons of the ruling power, and to spy upon the prince with whom they were school-fellows. If it is Rosencrantz who gives expression to the notion of the interrelatedness of ruler and ruled it is Guildenstern who asseverates:

> Most holy and religious fear it is
> To keep those many many bodies safe

That live and feed upon your Majesty.
(III. iii. 10)

Their observations about the centrality of rulers in their society may be true enough, but in having the two young men speak in this way to a ruler who is, as the audience knows, totally self-interested, the play underlines the speciousness of such arguments when they are used to justify all kinds of behaviour. This implies a ready acceptance of whatever it is that the state demands of the individual; a multitude of sins may be committed in the name of the security of the state and the preservation of order. Moreover, the security of the rule of a man like Claudius, and the task of defending it is invested, by Guildenstern's language — 'holy and religious' — with the aura of religious sanctity. As we know such a habit is only too noticeable in the verbal practice of certain twentieth-century governments. An extreme example of this, but nevertheless pertinent, may be found in the comment which Dr Verwoerd made in a broadcast to his people after recovering from the first assassination attempt upon his life:

I trust that I will be permitted to testify to my conviction that the protection of Divine Providence was accorded one with a purpose, a purpose which concerns South Africa too. May it be given me to fulfil that task faithfully.[21]

His view was endorsed by his supporters, as evidenced by the pro-government newspaper *Die Burger* which wrote: 'In this miraculous escape, all believers will see the hand of God himself.'[22]

The play shows that the failure of men such as Polonius, Rosencrantz, and Guildenstern to think about their world and their actions, their ready conformity to the wishes of the powerful, and their willingness to compromise their own integrity implicates them by default in a process of domination from which they are not themselves safe. All three, in the course of pursuing their ruler's wishes, are destroyed.

Because of their innocence of the really destructive force to which they minister, these servants of the King are especially interesting to audiences in South Africa. In this context too, we may recall the case of Adolph Eichmann. It may be true that his experience provides the best example of the consequences of action on behalf of a self-interested order ready to take any measures to deal with that which is different from it. Although Eichmann claimed diminished responsibility for his actions, he carried out the policies of his superior, and has been seen to be culpable for that. But it may be argued that, despite his legal argument at his trial, Eichmann was fairly well informed about the nature of his work, and more obviously, was an active and willing participant in the role assigned him. The position of Polonius, Rosencrantz and Guildenstern is more interesting to some of us precisely because of their genuine innocence of the King's hidden evil. We may remember the innocence that some of us have claimed in southern Africa, not necessarily because we believe that we disagree with what is happening or because we do not know about what is happening, but because we claim we have no power over what is happening. True as this may be, the unquestioning acceptance which results is not very different from the unquestioning acceptance with which Polonius, Rosencrantz and Guildenstern obey their king. It is true that the three have very little alternative, they can hardly disobey an absolute monarch when he asks them to serve him, just as in southern Africa it has been very difficult for some genuine dissenters to find a means of confronting the dominant order. But in *Hamlet* such qualifications in no way free the dramatic characters from the process of dishonesty and destruction that eventually includes them. Moreover we know that silence and compliance has its rewards, and the recipients, as Hamlet on one occasion has it, are to be compared to a 'sponge' that 'soaks up the King's countenance, his rewards, his authorities . . .' (IV. ii. 15). Christopher Hope has written pointedly about the lives of similar beneficiaries in southern Africa:

> In the foyer a sugar baron's rifles rust,
> they've not been pulled through in years.
> In the bar, bottle tops shower the wooden slats

which save the floor, hiding slopped beers
and totwash sluiced away. Two cricket bats
in the umbrella stand unpeel the smell of linseed.
In the lavatory someone is hawking phlegm.
A planter declares the Zulu a broken nation.
Rumour has it there are some so rich
they allow the air-conditioning to breathe for them
and employ servants merely for observation.[23]

The Hungarian writer, George Konrad, it is worth noting, has observed that 'the true symbol of the totalitarian state is not the executioner but the exemplary bureaucrat who proves to be more loyal to the state than to his friend.'[24]

4

Roland Mushat Frye points out that various characteristics attached to Claudius suggest certain sixteenth- and seventeenth-century versions of the traits of the tyrannous ruler. Whitney's *A Choice of Emblems*, for instance, presents a visualisation of the tyrant and the sponge, pointing to the tyrant's exploitation of dependent flatterers.[25] Claudius's use of 'Switzers' (IV. v. 97), he argues, recalls the fact that, as Erasmus noted, mercenaries were considered the necessary choice for any tyrant:

the tyrant guarantees safety for himself by means of foreign attendants and hired brigands. The king deems himself safe through his kindness to his subjects and their love for him in return.[26]

Furthermore, Cladius's fear of Hamlet's popularity amongst the people may bespeak the tyrant's fear of being supplanted. His entire mode of ruling seems summarised, argues Frye, by 'one of the most influential political theorists of the later sixteenth century', George Buchanan:

tyrants, cherishing the false appearance of a kingdom, when by fair means or foul they have once obtained it, cannot hold it without crime, nor can they give it up without destroying it.[27]

In addition to this, *Hamlet* pays particular attention to the use of surveillance and spying as a means of control. Moreover, Shakespeare shows that a government such as that of Claudius with its capacity to manipulate men such as Polonius, Rosencrantz and Guildenstern, depends not only upon spying but in the end also upon violence to retain that control.

Acts II and III are partly structured around the activity of spying. The procurement of spies is demonstrated in Act II scenes i and ii, the business of spying in Act II scene ii and Act III scene ii, and the report back by informants to their 'instigator' in Act II scene ii and Act III scene i.[28] Hamlet comments directly on the corrupting effect that such methods of government bespeak when he replies to Guildenstern's admission that he cannot play the recorder:

Why, look you now, how unworthy a thing you make of me. You would play upon me, you would seem to know my stops, you would pluck out the heart of my mystery, you would sound me from my lowest note to the top of my compass; and there is much music, excellent voice, in this little organ, yet cannot you make it speak. 'Sblood, do you think I am easier to be played on than a pipe? Call me what instrument you will, though you fret me, you cannot play upon me.

(III. ii. 363)

The denial of human dignity and trust which the practice of spying entails, and the consequent reduction of the human subject to an object solely of exploitation is something of which Hamlet is well aware — even as he asserts the precious integrity, 'much music, excellent voice', of the inner life of the individual which ought not to be so recklessly or ruthlessly ignored.

Hamlet concentrates especially in Act IV upon the inherent violence in Denmark's ruler, which surfaces when his self-interest is threatened. At the same time the text demonstrates the increasing disruption that Claudius's method of government produces in the social order. Claudius's self-interest is apparent in Act IV scene i when he deliberately reinforces Gertrude's alarm over the death of Polonius, hoping perhaps to prepare her for the planned murder of her son (IV. i. 12—15). Even as he speaks, it is clear that Claudius's mind runs continually to the political implication for himself of what has happened (IV. i. 16—19, 38—45). When he reappears in the third scene, the text presents him as actively persuading the court of the 'justice' of his action in removing the prince, heir to the throne (IV. iii. 1—11). Then, when on his own, he reveals his real, murderous intentions.

The play also shows that for Claudius, the consequences of his actions prove uncontrollable. Polonius, the first overt casualty of this spy-ridden order, is followed soon after by another casualty, his daughter. When Claudius encounters her madness directly on stage, he broods about the implications such developments have for his position. From what he says, it is clear that the effect of his rule and its consequences now impinge upon the consciousnesses of his subjects. The people, he muses, are 'muddied,/Thick and unwholesome in their thoughts and whispers/For good Polonius' death' (IV. v. 83). They are concerned too about the 'hugger-mugger' (IV. v. 84) behaviour of their rulers. The process of destabilisation continues when Laertes, returning from abroad and convinced Claudius is responsible for his father's death, makes his way to the King, while, in the words of the messenger:

> The rabble call him lord,
> And, as the world were now but to begin,
> Antiquity forgot, custom not known —
> The ratifiers and props of every word —
> They cry, 'Choose we! Laertes shall be king.'
> Caps, hands and tongues applaud it to the clouds,
> 'Laertes shall be king, Laertes king.'
>
> (IV. v. 108)

The text confirms Claudius's great persuasive skills as politician and the immensely destructive effect of that skill and its self-interested centre upon those around him most explicitly in the encounter between the King and Laertes. Claudius deflects the reckless animus of the young Laertes, redirecting it against Hamlet. He encourages Laertes to an act of revenge which, as critics have noted, commits him to 'damnable' action.[29] The play provides here a rich image of the poisonous ruler corrupting his subject, for Laertes, in agreeing to Claudius's plans, becomes himself an agent of the ruler's thrust to maintain his dominant position.

5

This depiction of the process of spying and violence in the play suggests, however, more than simply the tyranny of Claudius. The King refers to the 'muddied' and 'unwholesome' thoughts of the populace. The messenger emphasises that members of the subordinate order are voicing support for Laertes as antagonist to the King. Both speakers assume the ready agreement of the court as a whole to the undesirability of any involvement of the subordinate classes in events. These brief references offer a glimpse of the ruling class's attitude to those it dominates; but its own claims to legitimacy and natural rights of government, its claim moreover to class (and national) unity of purpose is brought into question in the events of *Hamlet*, not merely by those aspects of surveillance that the play foregrounds, but precisely by the fact that the text is directly concerned with antagonisms within the dominant order. Thus although it is true that almost no other attention is given to the subordinate classes in the play, the text conveys a distinct uneasiness about the real nature of the ruling class. This unease is clearly present in the central situation where two 'mighty opposites' (V. ii. 62) confront one another. Claudius, king within the dominant order, is threatened or opposed by the second most powerful individual within that order — the prince who has right of inheritance to the throne. Later, for a short while, Claudius is challenged too by Laertes. Moreover, the fact that the young Hamlet is confronted by the ghost of his father who confirms that he was victim of his own brother's ambitions implies that such antagonisms within the ruling class are not particularly new. We may recall the brief observation made at the beginning of this chapter about the actuality of antagonisms within the Elizabethan dominant order. In this context Lawrence Stone emphasises that everything depended upon Elizabeth's particular skills:

At court and throughout the central administration, Elizabeth spent her reign walking the tightrope, balancing one noble faction off against another, and the Essex Revolt was the only occasion in forty years when the royal acrobat slipped. 'The principall note of her raigne,' remarked Naunton, 'will be that she ruled much by faction and parties, which she her selfe both made, upheld, and weakned as her owne great judgement advised.'[30]

Claudius's decisions at the beginning of the play might reflect just such a need to strengthen and weaken faction, as *his* judgement devises. Thus Laertes is favoured and promoted over the Hamlet whom he suspects and who must, accordingly, be restrained under the watchful eye of the Danish court. Rosencrantz and Guildenstern understand their brief from the King as one which requires discovery of the exact nature of Hamlet's ambitions. And certain of the points which Frye argues about Hamlet's recognition, just before he kills the King, that Denmark is an elective monarchy, suggest a sensitivity of the text to its own subversive implications about antagonism within the dominant order. These in turn are held in check to prevent the play and presumably the players from falling foul of the censor and the authorities.

Frye argues that 'in England the hereditary principle was so strong that most Englishmen would have assumed Claudius to be a usurper until they were told in the last scene that the Danish monarchy was elective.'[31] Hamlet says, at that point:

Does it not, think thee, stand me now upon —
He that hath kill'd my king and whor'd my mother,
Popp'd in between th'election and my hopes,
Thrown out his angle for my proper life
And with such coz'nage — is't not perfect conscience
To quit him with this arm? And is't not to be damn'd
To let this canker of our nature come
In further evil?

(V. ii. 70)

In this context, Frye recalls Bishop Thomas Bilson's work, *The True Difference between Christian Subjection and Unchristian Rebellion* commissioned by Queen Elizabeth and issued three times between 1585 and 1595. It suggests that although a hereditary monarch who becomes a tyrant may be opposed, he may not be deposed, whereas elective monarchs who are tyrannous may be removed.[32] Frye suggests that, although Shakespeare's company had been exonerated over their performance of *Richard II* just before the Essex uprising, nevertheless:

to present the killer of a king as a sympathetic character could entail misunderstanding . . . Shakespeare introduced the fact that Denmark was an elective monarchy just before . . . and . . . shortly after the king's death. [Thus] Shakespeare . . . presented Hamlet in a more favourable way while protecting himself and his company from the danger of dramatising a scene in which a sympathetic and attractive hero kills a crowned king. Should the authorities object, the Lord Chamberlain's men could point to the official Elizabethan doctrine as presented by Bishop Bilson.[33]

This resonance of unease in the text about possible disruption within the dominant order is most evident in the presentation of Hamlet himself. The prince is portrayed as a young man adhering to traditional values of human justice and right action. In one sense this depiction of Hamlet, located in a world he considers unjust at its core, has obvious point for many twentieth-century audiences — Hamlet's 'integrity' is reflected in his manifest concern with the problem of action in the play. The profundity of this concern to understand himself and his world, to act with honour against the trend of ruthless violence in the social order emerges from everything he says, and especially from his soliloquies: the fluctuating emotions, contradictions, and the violent as well as the rational thoughts to which he is given, bear witness to the intensity of his endeavour.[34] This 'integrity' in Hamlet is established especially in language that draws on Christian discourse, evident in the moral undercurrents in his satirical awareness, in his ability to speak not only for the general but for the particular and personal in human experience, and in his capacity for and concern with human feeling — all of which contrast powerfully with the ruler of Denmark and those who work for him. At the same time the play seems to bring into question the effectiveness of these traditional values within the realities of the social order, itself undergoing increasing change — dramatically hinted at by the sudden transference of power from the old to the new monarch at the beginning of the play. Thus Hamlet, who believes in those doctrines and especially their underlying Christian thrust which the ruler himself uses to legitimate his position of domination within the social order, is brought by these very same doctrines into a position of antagonism towards, and confrontation with, his monarch.

6

Although it expresses unease, the play does not hint at an effective means of eradicating those problems it identifies. Indeed, *Hamlet* offers, in the death of Claudius, only an apparent resolution to those elements in the play which register disturbing aspects in the operation of state power, and those elements which identify the existence of tensions and antagonisms within the dominant order. For one thing, despite all that Hamlet's own language about action suggests in terms of traditional Christian discourse — and despite the final death of Claudius — those less deliberately exploitative than the King, and especially Hamlet himself, are dead too. Moreover the Fortinbras who replaces him, is, in certain senses at least, as committed to force as his predecessor. And a sense of the indifference of agents of state power is generated in one of Hamlet's soliloquies by the lines which recognise the Norwegian prince's callously exploitative attitude to the subordinate orders. In battle he is happy to countenance:

The imminent death of twenty thousand men
That, for a fantasy and trick of fame,

> Go to their graves like beds, fight for a plot
> Whereon the numbers cannot try the cause,
> Which is not tomb enough and continent
> To hide the slain . . .

(IV. iv. 66)

Hamlet appears to respond to these various problems only by stressing enigma and mystery. These are the conditions within which the tragic loss of those who believe in traditional notions of goodness and justice occurs. The indeterminacy and mystery of these deaths, particularly, contribute to the play's assertion of tragedy. We should further note that in scrutinising human action in this way, *Hamlet* places it, intermittently, in the context of Christian discourse and in the context of the uncontrollable factor of accident in a fallen world.

Hamlet's accidental slaying of Polonius is only one of a string of uncontrollable incidents or indications in the text that appear to assert the significance of accident as a factor affecting the realisation of human intentions in action. Claudius's plan to murder Hamlet is partly undone by the accident of Hamlet's discovery of the letter on board the ship carrying him to England, as well as the chance attack by pirates. The emphasis upon death in the first scene of Act V not only acknowledges its finality but, in the detailed texture of the language, underlines the limits of human endeavour — 'Imperious Caesar, dead and turn'd to clay,/Might stop a hole to keep the wind away' (V. i. 207). And in the final scene, the text presents at last that action about which the whole play has been concerned. It offers, in the duel itself, a powerful dramatic enactment of accident and of the proposition that man cannot in action anticipate or control the outcome of his intentions. Claudius, in the presence of a compliant Gertrude, a Laertes who has become his tool, and a court largely supportive of his rule and unaware of its evil, attempts to implement the murder of Hamlet, but the unpredictability of experience appears to dominate. Hamlet dies but Gertrude, Laertes, and the King himself meet their death as well. Or, to put this more appropriately, although the

44

poisonous ruler is finally killed, many others die in the process. Hamlet may in the penultimate scenes of the play
recognise a 'divinity that shapes our ends' (V. ii. 10) but this
must be set against the 'quarry' that 'cries on havoc'
(V. ii. 369) concluding it. The sweet prince whose heroic consciousness, more than any other in the play, has sought
goodness and justice dies even as he frees the kingdom of
its unjust ruler. The sense of loss at this — 'Now cracks a
noble heart' (V. ii. 364) — at the text's end, includes the
acknowledgement of mystery of a kind too profound, apparently, to be reducible to any one system or explanation —
as Hamlet, dying, has it, 'the rest is silence' (V. ii. 363).

7

I remarked in the first chapter that traditional Anglo-
American approaches to the Shakespeare text were never
so narrow as the South African version of them. Thus location of that language in *Hamlet* relating to accident and
mystery, ultimately perceived in terms of traditional Christian discourse, is rare in South African criticism. This narrowness is in part a consequence of the determination to react to
tragedy primarily in terms of character; it is also, as I briefly
hinted in chapter 1, 'Shakespeare Depoliticised', the result of
the South African habit of treating the Shakespeare text as a
particular kind of 'moral gymnasium'. This approach endeavours continually to turn the Shakespeare text to use in order
to detect and inculcate certain appropriate attitudes, the possession of which constitutes the right kind of 'self-improvement'. Thus, another South African critic writing on *Hamlet*
observes in the course of his discussion:

we read literature, presumably, at least in part, to grow: by entering
into a vision of life that is not our own we extend our awareness and
our capacity, and a commitment to a particular approach should not be
such as to preclude the possibility of literature changing us.[35]

His version of what such self-improvement and growth might
entail, however, is not as liberating as his avoidance of

'recourse to the logic of the whole [as] the authoritative determinant of interpretation' (p. 87) might promise. Indeed his procedure suggests little more than a skilful re-enactment (and by implication advocation) of a version of New Criticism. He poses as alternative interpretations of Act V scene i lines 239—256, either 'the prince's striving for and ultimately finding an adequate role in terms of which to perform a called-for action' or what he calls 'the sickness at the heart of life' (p. 87) and eventually concludes:

If one had hitherto been preoccupied with the sense of Hamlet's searching for an appropriate role or mode of action, one would have to ensure . . . that that hypothesis was broad enough to include the tragic necessity of surrendering other more devoutly-to-be-wished roles . . . which would not have left a man with a sense of 'how ill all's here about my heart.' If, to take another example, one had been preoccupied with the sense of Hamlet's coming to terms with the sickness at heart of life, one would have to ensure that the hypothesis was broad enough to include the dignity of finding stature and purpose in the very heart of loss (pp. 89—90).

Although the discussion appears to reject a unitary response to the play, the alternative possibilities it postulates prove to be different versions of the same emphasis — both foreground aspects of human nature and action as these may be deduced from the character Hamlet alone.

But the concern with accident in the language and situation of *Hamlet* develops in a way that moves beyond such narrowness of focus. Rather than leading to perceptions enabling a certain kind of attitude to or conclusions about human nature and action that will allow us to 'grow', the text, in its scrutiny of action encounters complexity, difficulty and problem. And even within traditional frameworks of response, set against such narrowness in the South African traditional approach, we may discern a different version of the tragedy. In his book, *The Unnatural Scene,* Michael Long identifies some notions of Schopenhauer, although he applies these in ways different from that aspect I consider here. [36] Long connects the concerns of Shakespeare's tragedies with Schopenhauer's observation that tragedy as well as comedy results from the consciousness's inability to control or even understand the world which it so limitedly captures in its concepts . . . here . . . is an idea of tragedy which sees it as central to the dynamics of mental and psychological life . . . comprehensible to a mind . . . fully apprised of a high energy world of on-going destructive power before which, at any moment, the mind may be rendered powerless (p. 16).

Such a force, continues Long, for Schopenhauer, 'made a destructive mockery of the human world which offered to understand or control it' (pp. 16—17). The 'tragic response' is proposed as one means of dealing with this view of experience. Long quotes from Schopenhauer on the impact of this tragic realisation:

we feel ourselves urged to turn our will away from life, to give up willing and loving life . . . we become convinced more clearly than ever that life is a bad dream from which we have to awake . . . the dawning of the knowledge that the world and life can afford no true satisfaction, and are therefore not worth our attachment to them. It is this that the tragic spirit consists [sic]; accordingly it leads to resignation (p. 17).

Schopenhauer's concern with the world as a refraction of the perceiving mind and his concept of the world as *die Wille* are not ideas which Shakespeare in any way shared.[37] However, the sense of the 'consciousness's inability to control or even understand the world which it so limitedly captures in its concepts' does, as Long seems to suggest, relate to a similar recognition, (naturally, amongst several others) in Shakespeare's play. The text's sense of the mysterious aspects of human experience, moreover, is expressed not merely through the acknowledgement of the fact of accident. The concern with human, individual endeavour, which we have no difficulty in identifying is often balanced in the language of the text against more overt recognition of the limited effectiveness of human action when set in a larger, apparently uncontrollable universe. Again the diverse nature of these attempts to describe or define action and its outcome in the play intensifies the sense of problem and mystery, which the text appears to assert as inevitably attendant upon any attempt to fathom the secret of human action.

Several of the lines given to the Player King, for example, argue the limitation of human action directly. The Player King tells the Queen:

> I do believe you think what now you speak;
> But what we do determine, oft we break.
> Purpose is but the slave to memory,
> Of violent birth but poor validity,
> Which now, the fruit unripe, sticks on the tree,
> But fall unshaken when they mellow be.
> Most necessary 'tis that we forget
> To pay ourselves what to ourselves is debt.
> What to ourselves in passion we propose,
> The passion ending, doth the purpose lose.
> . . . .
> Our wills and fates do so contrary run
> That our devices still are overthrown:
> Our thoughts are ours, their ends none of our own.
>
> (III. ii. 208)

Furthermore, Hamlet's consideration of action from a variety of perspectives contributes to this effect of mystery. His attempts may, admittedly, be read as his scrutiny of the possible ways of resisting or adopting an oppositional stance against the dominant power.[38] At the same time, in the multiplicity of attempts he makes, the difficulty of defining precisely the nature of human action is foregrounded. When, for instance he requests the Second Player to speak about the revenge of Phyrrus, it is clear the prince is considering action in the aspect of unrestrained violence, the end result of the revenge impulse (II. ii. 442—514). Then again, in conversation with Horatio, Hamlet contemplates commitment to the opposite kind of action, suggested by the capacity of his friend who, 'in suff'ring all . . . suffers nothing' (III. ii. 66). Hamlet says admiringly of this:

> Give me that man
> That is not passion's slave, and I will wear him
> In my heart's core, ay, in my heart of heart,
> As I do thee.
>
> (III. ii. 74)

At times, Hamlet appears motivated by the seventeenth-century sense of original sin, when, with bitterness, he refers to man's incapacity to act in love with any reliability — 'for virtue cannot so innoculate our old stock but we shall relish of it' (III. i. 118). But, by contrast again, in his discussion with Horatio about Danish drinking customs he laments the extent to which man's capacity for noble action can be underrated because of his imperfections. Man's natural limitations, suggests Hamlet, may be used to cloud the 'pith and marrow' (I. iv. 22) of what he does achieve.

In the detail of the language of other speakers too the imperfection of action in this world is delineated. The appearance of the Ghost in Act I scene i, starting like a 'guilty thing' (I. i. 153) prompts Marcellus to glimpse, by contrast with the world of the play, for a moment, a world at Christmas, closest to one without blemish when

> no spirit dare stir abroad,
> The nights are wholesome, then no planets strike,
> No fairy takes, nor witch hath power to charm,
> So hallow'd and so gracious is that time.
>
> (I. i. 169)

Laertes speaks to his sister of the world's imperfections in general terms, significantly with natural imagery, when he observes:

> Virtue itself scapes not calumnious strokes.
> The canker galls the infants of the spring
> Too oft before their buttons be disclos'd,
> And in the morn and liquid dew of youth
> Contagious blastments are most imminent.
>
> (I. iii. 42)

and his father, in seeking to know the imperfections of his son's behaviour in Paris, instructs Reynaldo to:

> breathe his faults so quaintly
> That they may seem the taints of liberty,
> The flash and outbreak of a fiery mind,

49

> A savageness in unreclaimed blood,
> Of general assault.

(II. i. 35)

The richness of the differing perspectives on human action and the varied attempts to account for it in *Hamlet,* then, also posit a mystery surrounding human endeavour as men struggle to comprehend and make sense of action in this world. Indeed, the darkness of the first scene together with the appearance of the Ghost, may be taken as two key images which direct the audience at once to the fact of the unknown and the mysterious in experience. It juxtaposes this recognition against an instinctive human need for knowledge and order, suggested in the eagerness of the dramatic characters to identify each other, their references to the order and rhythm of nature, the urgency with which they question the ghost, the relief, touched with religious reverence, with which they greet the dawn.

8

This resort to mystery as a means of accounting for tragic loss within an established but conflict ridden social order, seems present too in certain modern South African narratives. Sipho Sepamla's novel *The Root is One,*[39] for instance, tells the story of two young friends who at the commencement of the book are both concerned to struggle against a world which they consider to be unjust and oppressive. But in the course of events their intentions go awry. They become involved in a strike and attempt to form a resistance movement against the authority's plan to institute removals from their location and to demolish the dwellings which remain. By the end of the story there have been riots in protest at the removals, there has been bloodshed, and the bulldozers have moved in. One of the young men has been arrested and the other kills himself for having informed upon his friend to the ruling powers. Sepamla at the conclusion of the novel describes the reaction of the people of the location to these events:

50

The crowd waited: this crowd of women and children and a sprinkling of men. To kill the time, they began to chatter, to ask questions, to discover the truth they lived but were unable to articulate. They were turning themselves inside out; they were rubbing their sore spots in an effort to reduce to nothingness this huge hurt which followed their lives like the shadows tailing daylight. The dead were praised, the living were damned. In all they said, they hoped to reveal before their own eyes the meaning of their lives. But the mystery of it remained, only its particles were revealed in such events as the removals and the suicide of men.

Night was creeping in, confirming a dying — of men as well, and of the place. A sadness pervaded all moments. The sight of ruins had become common by nightfall — these ruins which some said were the extension of human decay.

Some things were said in whispers, others loudly. And in the process of it all someone summed up the tragedy of the moment: Spiwo was in jail awaiting serious charges; Juda was dead after saying he had let down his friend. Then it was asked: how was survival? Each of these young men had sought survival. Each had been harassed by the moment and, in a desperate bid for survival, had dug his own grave. How ought people to behave in order to attain certain survival? The question remained unanswered, for the 'black maria' was heard screaming from afar. Now the tension, which had held the people gathered in knots near the house of Baloyi, heightened. There had been moments when it had risen with the expectation of some development and dropped with the sighs of disappointment.

'Listen,' some man said in one group, 'I am not God to sit in judgement over the deeds of others. I've grown grey watching and seeing many people do wrong, and yet I've always come forward to bury these same people. It is our duty as human beings to do just that in the end. For, when an enemy has died, what harm can he do in the coffin? Tell me that, what harm, m'm?'

'He speaks the truth' added another.

Encouraged, the first speaker said: 'You see, I'm concerned with the pain which the living must endure, which must be carried in the hearts of the living for days on end. The pain of suffering is like mist: it settles on every home' (pp. 129—30).

In Sepamla's description, a similar concern for the personal as well as the more general sense of experience, as may be found in *Hamlet*, is evident. The crowd waits, aware in its own personal way of the need to 'ask questions, to discover the truth they lived but were unable to articulate', experiencing as always the 'sore spots' and 'huge hurt' of the life it is forced to live. Hamlet we should remember, with a murdered father and a political opponent who has 'Popp'd in between th'election and my hopes,' (V. ii. 65) speaks with precision about:

> Th'oppressor's wrong, the proud man's contumely,
> The pangs of dispriz'd love, the law's delay,
> The insolence of office, and the spurns
> That patient merit of th'unworthy takes,
>
> (III. i. 74) [40]

Sepamla's text, too, speaks of this — as the 'pain the living must endure' that 'settles on every home.' It identifies an impenetrable mystery in experience — 'only its particles were revealed in such events as the removals and the suicide of men.' And in the context, both of the problematic nature of human action and determined self-interest, Sepamla's text, like Shakespeare's, salutes the heroism of those prepared to 'take arms against a sea of troubles' (III. i. 59) and to search for just and good action.

9

Different levels of signification, then, more numerous than many traditional South African critics have been ready to admit, operate in *Hamlet.* The language that directs us towards values evident in Christian discourse occurs in a context that suggests the absence of these values, and also, disturbingly, their possible impotence. Hamlet's convictions, as we have seen, bring him into confrontation with the principal ruler of that order of which he is himself part, an order that appears in practice to operate in terms only of the retention and assertion of dominance, and moreover one that seems in practice to be riven by internal rivalry and conflict. Nevertheless, although the principal agent of that order is removed by the play's conclusion, no essential change appears to have occurred. The play's unease about the dominant order endures, despite its apparent attempt to contain this unease by the death of Claudius and by reference to accident and mystery in a fallen world.

We might note in this context that the emergence of the present South African social formation was not the instant product of the Afrikaner Nationalist accession to power in 1948. The increase in control by mining and agricultural capital in the early years of this century generated a process that would go on to include the Land Act of 1913, a whole web of detailed legislation such as that contained in the Apprenticeship Act and the Industrial Conciliation Act, the Native Administration Act of 1927 and the 1936 Herzog Bills. All these contributed to a system of relationships that was, again, intensified further after 1948. Similarly, despite the claims made about the potential of individual rulers to change the South African social formation at the time of their accession to powerful positions within the state apparatus, no essential change has in fact occurred — only the continuation of a particular process. This applies, indeed, to important aspects of the roles played by General Herzog and Jan Christiaan Smuts when they held positions of power as much as it does, more recently, to Prime Minister John Vorster and President P.W. Botha.[41]

We may note briefly too that *Hamlet* becomes particularly interesting to us precisely because of the uncertainty it suggests about that world which has produced it. If we detect the hint of a recognition in *Hamlet* that the dominant classes perpetuate their own position despite changes in individual rulers, and we are aware of the unease about this with which the play ends, this is because such unease points to the conflicting and contradictory forces in the late Elizabethan world as it experienced movement from a feudal society to the beginnings of a capitalist society. And when we seek direct evidence of these forces we encounter descriptions of a social order, which, inevitably, includes as well as other factors we have already registered, different class-political divisions. One version of these may be cited here:

The Catholic position was associated with attempts to support a traditional conception of social hierarchy with the monarch representing the epitome of the social power of the aristocracy, in a system based on qualification by blood, stable wealth in land, and rule by personal domination; while the Protestant position was associated with a 'levelling' tendency in which the sovereign was coming to represent a rational conception of necessary social order, in a system based on qualification by moral legitimacy, expanding wealth in money, and rule by popular recognition or even consent. King James's watchword, 'No bishops no king' succinctly captured the fear of radical Protestantism, and the intensifying ideological-political bind in which the English monarchy found itself as a result of Henry VIII's actions in tying the fate of the institution to the developing Reformation — actions which, ironically, were meant to, and in the short run did, strengthen the power of the monarchy itself against the aristocracy and the Church.[42]

Such observations may point the way forward for us as we attempt, increasingly, to study the Shakespeare text as a signifying practice that is, most importantly, located in the material struggles taking place within the social order from which it comes.[43]

I would argue therefore that the young men and women in Soweto and elsewhere in South Africa, who know they are living in a system which is less than just, despite its official claims, will recognise many aspects of the situation depicted in *Hamlet*. They will respond to the unease we may detect in the text about the working of state power within the social order, an unease which the resort in the language to accident, mystery and an imperfect world, does not dissipate. Furthermore, if they themselves care about justice they will understand Hamlet's anger at a society that compromises with injustice and they will share his agony at the problem of finding the proper action that will at last realise that justice. They will also know, distressingly, that the 'pain of living' is often the pain of a Horatio, who at the end of the play understands, as does Sipho Sepamla, that it is more and more frequently the dead who must be praised. They, most of all, have cared and because they have challenged injustice they have died. Not all such men and women may be interested in Shakespeare, but the experience of *Hamlet* is in their blood.

Notes

1 All references to *Hamlet* in this chapter are taken from *Hamlet* ed. Harold Jenkins (London: Methuen, 1982). References are to act, scene, and line. Where more than one line is quoted, the number for the 'last' quoted line is given.

2 Muriel Horrell ed., *Survey of Race Relations in South Africa 1981,* (Johannesburg: South African Institute of Race Relations, 1982) pp. 85—6.

3 B.L. Joseph, *Shakespeare's Eden* (London: Blandford Press, 1971), p. 197. The short essay by J. Hurstfield, 'The Historical and Social Background' in *A New Companion to Shakespeare Studies,* ed. K. Muir and S. Schoenbaum (Cambridge: Cambridge University Press, 1971), still provides a useful summary of some main features of the period.

4 Jan Kott, *Shakespeare Our Contemporary* (London: Methuen, 1975), p. 48.

5 Dollimore and Sinfield, 'History and Ideology: the instance of *Henry V'*, p. 219

6 Bevington, *Tudor Drama and Politics,* p. 25.

7 Quoted in John D'Oliveira, *Vorster the Man* (Johannesburg: Ernest Stanton Publisher, 1977), pp. 157—8.

8 A brief and clear statement of the problem posed by the revenge ethic is to be found in Winifred Nowottny's article on 'Shakespeare's Tragedies' in *Shakespeare's World*, ed. J. Hurstfield and J. Sutherland (London: Edward Arnold, 1964), pp. 48—78.

9 Hamlet himself comments on this, for instance in II. ii. 594—99.

10 Roland Mushat Frye, *The Renaissance Hamlet: Issues and Responses in 1600* (Princeton: Princeton University Press, 1984). I am totally indebted in the discussion which follows to Frye, especially, for the immediate discussion, to chapters 2 and 3, pp. 11—75.

11 Frye, *The Renaissance Hamlet,* p. 12.

12 Frye, *The Renaissance Hamlet,* p. 50.

13 Cited in Frye, *The Renaissance Hamlet,* p. 48.

14 Frye, *The Renaissance Hamlet,* pp. 49—50. Frye quotes from this sermon: 'As the king's majesty may not attribute his right unto the crown, but unto God and unto his father, who hath not only given him grace to be born into the world, but also to govern as a king in the world; whose right and title the crown confirmeth, and sheweth the same unto all the world. Whereas this right by God

and natural succession precedeth, not the coronation, the ceremony availeth nothing. A traitor may receive the crown, and yet [be a] true king nothing the rather. So an hypocrite and [an] infidel may receive the external sign of baptism and yet no christian man nothing the rather.'

15 Cited in Frye, *The Renaissance Hamlet*, p. 30. Aquinas wrote: 'He who takes vengeance on the wicked in keeping with his rank and position does not usurp what belongs to God, but makes use of the power granted him by God' (p. 31).

16 Frye, *The Renaissance Hamlet*, pp. 31–7.

17 Frye, *The Renaissance Hamlet*, p. 264.

18 Nigel Alexander, *Poison, Play and Duel* (London: Routledge and Kegan Paul, 1971), pp. 51–2, writes: 'in his opening speech Claudius displays a firm and impressive grasp of . . . rhetoric. In a series of striking phrases, he combines ideas of opposite meaning in an attempt to persuade his audience that, having weighed the arguments, he is pursuing a reasonable course of action. The rhetoric thus conceals the fact that his forceful and aggressive behaviour is based only upon one of the opposed views which he mentions.'

19 There are numerous articles dealing with Polonius's use of proverbs. For opposing views see K. Lever, 'Proverbs and *Sententiae* in the plays of Shakespeare', *The Shakespeare Association Bulletin* 13, 1938, pp. 173–83, 224–39 and Doris V. Falk, 'Proverbs and the Polonius Destiny', *Shakespeare Quarterly* 18, 1967, pp. 23–36. See also, Joan Bennet, 'Characterization in Polonius's advice to Laertes', *Shakespeare Quarterly* 4, 1953, pp. 3–9. The best comments on the subject are made by Leonard F. Dean, 'Shakespeare's treatment of conventional ideas', *The Sewanee Review* 52, 1944, pp. 414–23.

20 Molly Mahood, *Shakespeare's Wordplay* (London: Methuen, 1968), has valuable observations about the language in this scene, pp. 119–28.

21 Broadcast to the South African people on 20 May 1960; quoted in Henry Kenney, *Architect of Apartheid* (Johannesburg: Jonathan Ball, 1980), p. 195.

22 Kenney, *Architect of Apartheid*, p. 195.

23 Christopher Hope, *In the Country of the Black Pig* (Johannesburg: Ravan, 1981). From the poem 'The Country Club', p. 3.

24 George Konrad, 'The Long Work of Liberty', *The New York Review of Books*, 26 January 1978, p. 28.

25 Frye, *The Renaissance Hamlet*, p. 39.

26 Cited in Frye, *The Renaissance Hamlet*, p. 38.

27 Cited in Frye, *The Renaissance Hamlet*, p. 38.

28 Ophelia, who does not realise the implications of her behaviour, dutifully reports to her father about Hamlet, in effect, because of the use Polonius makes of what he is told, informing on the prince to the ruler.

29 Nigel Alexander, *Poison, Play and Duel*, writes: 'Laertes . . . is prepared to violate sanctuary . . . The contrast between this desire to prove oneself in "deed" and Hamlet, who has spent the play, prayer, and closet scenes anatomizing his role as his father's son in words is deliberate and striking . . . [The King's] appeal to conscience persuades Laertes to take part in an act which, if he had time to think and reflect, he would find against his conscience' (p. 191).

30 Lawrence Stone, *The Crisis of the Aristocracy 1558–1641* (Oxford: Oxford University Press, 1965) pp. 256–7.

31 Frye, *The Renaissance Hamlet*, p. 263.

32 Frye, *The Renaissance Hamlet*, p. 265.

33 Frye, *The Renaissance Hamlet*, p. 266, 265.

34 The point is often made about Hamlet that he refuses to choose the way of compromise, the way of the rash force of a Fortinbras, or the way of the thoughtless passion of a Laertes who ends by serving the designs of a wicked ruler.

35 B.D. Cheadle, 'Hamlet at the Graveside: A Leap into Hermeneutics', *English Studies in Africa*, 22:2, 1979, pp. 83–90, p. 87.

36 Michael Long, *The Unnatural Scene* (London: Methuen, 1976).

37 In referring to these terms I rely upon the use made of them by Long in his book.

38 Frye, *The Renaissance Hamlet*, pp. 188–93, for example, argues that Hamlet's question 'whether 'tis nobler in the mind to suffer/ The slings and arrows of outrageous fortune/Or to take arms against a sea of troubles/And by opposing end them' (III. i. 57–60) 'could not have been raised in 1600 as though in some hermetically sealed philosophical isolation, because it was fundamental and divisive throughout Western Europe in the latter third of the sixteenth century . . . prominent Jesuits recommended violent action when necessary to achieve virtuous ends, and prominent Calvinists in France, Holland and Scotland, not only advocated but actually did take arms against a "sea of troubles", and by opposing did in some sense end them, overturning regimes and replacing monarchs by their own combination of activism and faith.' He draws interesting parallels to Donne's 'Satyre III' lines 77–84 and to Queen Elizabeth I 'as she sat in gloomy isolation and wavered back and forth

over what to do about Mary Stuart . . . It might be necessary and one's moral duty to strike down a crowned sovereign, but it was not morally easy, even when one already wore a crown oneself.'

39 Sipho Sepamla, *The Root is One* (London: Rex Collings, 1979).
40 See Harold Jenkins, ed., *Hamlet*, note on I. ii. 1, pp. 433–4.
41 See for instance H.J. Simons and R.E. Simons, *Class and Colour in South Africa 1850–1950* (Harmondsworth: Penguin, 1969).
42 Note to James H. Kavanagh, 'Shakespeare in Ideology' in Drakakis, *Alternative Shakespeares*, pp. 144–65, p. 233.
43 For further clarification see Catherine Belsey, *Critical Practice* (London: Methuen, 1980) and Catherine Belsey, *The Subject of Tragedy* (London: Methuen, 1985).

3 *Othello* and the 'plain face' of Racism

Solomon T. Plaatje did not come to Shakespeare's plays with the same perspective as those held, no doubt, by most of his contemporary counterparts within the white ruling group of South Africa. But he responded to significant aspects of Shakespeare more reliably than they. Plaatje, who translated several of the works, including *Othello,* into Tswana, observed that 'Shakespeare's dramas . . . show that nobility and valour, like depravity and cowardice, are not the mono-poly of any colour.'[1]

Before Plaatje's time *Othello* had been, during the nine-teenth century, one of the most popular plays at the Cape. But a personal advertisement published before an 1836 performance suggests the gulf that lay between Plaatje's sentiment and what is likely to have been the opinion of inhabitants in 1836:

In frequenting the Theatre, do not professing Christians pointedly violate their baptismal vows? . . . In listening to Othello, do they not necessarily contract a horrible familiarity with passions and deeds of the most fiendish character . . . and give up their minds to be polluted by language so gross? Is not the guilt of such persons great, and their danger imminent?[2]

When the play was translated into Dutch because of its popularity, it was given the title *Othello of De Jaloersche Zwart* — 'Othello or the Jealous Black.'[3]

The absence or presence of racist attitudes in any critic inevitably determines his reading of the text, as the differ-ence between Plaatje's remark and the comment of the writer in nineteenth-century South Africa demonstrates. Indeed, study of the play in South Africa today still produces prob-lems. Moreover, in the case of *Othello* serious difficulties extend beyond criticism within what at present remains the *apartheid* state. Not only the traditional South African approach, but also certain currents in traditionalist Anglo-American criticism have, alarmingly, preferred a narrow concern with interiority, with often equivocal and disturbing emphasis upon Othello himself.

The tasks for students approaching the text are manifold. We need to identify the attitudes to colour, so far as these can be determined, in Shakespeare's age. We need also to determine the attitude to colour in *Othello*. We need to take into account traditional readings that are not racist, but we also need to consider other ways in which the play reflects and interacts with the world from which it comes. And we need, finally, to address directly the problem of the *Othello* criticism that is itself inscribed by colour prejudice. As I will argue, these multiple activities continually reveal or confirm in the text a strong antipathy to all kinds of racism.

1

The English encounter with Africans began from about the mid-sixteenth century. Native West Africans had probably first appeared in London in 1554; certainly, as Eldred Jones points out, by 1601 there were enough black men in London to prompt Elizabeth to express her discontent 'at the great number of "Negars and blackamoors" which are crept into the realm since the troubles between her Highness and the King of Spain.'[4] In turn, Englishmen visited Africa in significant numbers in the second half of the sixteenth century, primarily for reasons of trade.[5]

As such scholars as Eldred Jones and Winthrop Jordan have taught us, there is ample evidence of the existence of colour prejudice in the England of Shakespeare's day. This prejudice may be accounted for in a number of ways, including xenophobia — as one proverb first recorded in the early seventeenth century has it, 'Three Moors to a Portuguese, three Portuguese to an Englishman' — as well as what V.G. Kiernan sees as a general tendency in the European encounter with Africa, namely, to see Africa as the barbarism against which European civilisation defined itself:

Revived memories of antiquity, the Turkish advance, the new horizons opening beyond, all encouraged Europe to see itself afresh as civilization confronting barbarism . . . Colour, as well as culture, was coming to be a distinguishing feature of Europe.[6]

Furthermore, as Winthrop Jordan argues, the Protestant Reformation in England, with its emphasis upon personal piety and intense self-scrutiny and internalised control, facilitated the tendency evidenced in Englishmen to use people overseas as 'social mirrors'.[7] Referring to the 'dark mood of strain and control in Elizabethan culture', Jordan highlights too the Elizabethan concern with the need for 'external self discipline' in a context of social ferment and change

caused in large part by an increasingly commercialized economy and reflected in such legislative monuments as the Statute of Apprentices and the Elizabethan vagrancy and poor laws . . . Literate Englishmen . . . were concerned with the apparent disintegration of social and moral controls at home; they fretted endlessly over the 'masterless men' who had once had a proper place in the social order but who were now wandering about, begging, robbing, raping. They fretted also about the absence of a spirit of due subordination — of children to parents and servants to masters. They assailed what seemed a growing spirit of avariciousness (p. 24).

Such Englishmen were on occasion inclined to discover attributes in others 'which they found first, but could not speak of, in themselves' (pp. 22—3).

These tendencies were coupled with a tradition of colour prejudice that scholars identify in the literature and iconography of Shakespeare's day and earlier.[8] Hunter provides a list of instances in literature which suggest that there was 'a powerful, widespread, and ancient tradition associating black-faced men with wickedness, and this tradition came right up to Shakespeare's own day' (p. 142). The habit of representing pictorially evil men as black faced or negroid persisted from the middle ages to beyond the sixteenth century. Several of the tormentors — although we should reiterate, not all — of Christ or other saints depicted on Church walls, windows or in certain of the Psalters have black faces. And before the sixteenth century, the meaning of the word 'black' as the

Oxford English Dictionary indicates, included a whole range of negative associations.[9]

Such factors may help to account for the white impulse to regard black men in set ways. Hunter notes that many pageants were led by black men who appeared to act as 'bogey man figures' to clear the way for the main procession.[10] In Jonson's 'Masque of Blackness' the colour black was depicted as less desirable than white.[11] Dark skinned Moors in plays were dramatised as cruel and wicked: Muly Hamet in Peele's *The Battle of Alcazar* was followed by Aaron in *Titus Andronicus* and Eleazar in *Lust's Dominion.*[12]

In travel writing, English ethnocentrism fastened upon differences in colour, religion, and style of life. Eldred Jones has assembled material that shows that Elizabethan Englishmen saw the natives of Africa as barbarous, treacherous, libidinous, and jealous. An account of the inhabitants along 'the coast of Guinea and the mydde partes of Africa,' for example, observes that they

were in oulde tyme called Ethiopes and Nigrite, which we nowe caule Moores, Moorens or Negros, a people of beastly lyvynge, without a god, lawe, religion or common welth and so scorched and vexed with the heate of the soone, that in many places they curse it when it ryseth.[13]

The treachery of black men was popularised in George Peele's play, *The Battle of Alcazar* (1588)[14]; their libidinousness was exemplified in William Waterman's *Fardle of Facions* (1555), which noted of the Icthiophagi that, after their meals, 'they falle uppon their women even as they come to hande withoute any choyse.'[15] And John Leo's *History and Description of Africa* (trans. 1600) presents the somewhat conflicting claim that black men are extremely jealous:

whomsoever they finde but talking with their wives they presently go about to murther them . . . by reason of jealousie you may see them daily one to be the death and destruction of another, . . . they will by no meanes match themselves unto an harlot.[16]

62

2

What evidence is there in *Othello* that the play shares the colour prejudice apparent in certain of the attitudes current in Shakespeare's age? Within the play racist sentiment is largely confined to Iago, Roderigo and Brabantio.[17] Both Iago and Roderigo use racist insinuation during their *putsch* against Othello's position and reputation. Iago tells Roderigo to wake Desdemona's father and his household so that he may 'incense her kinsmen,/And though he in a fertile climate dwell,/Plague him with flies' (I. i. 71).[18] A moment later as we know, he calls up to Brabantio that 'an old black ram/Is tupping your white ewe' (I. i. 89) and that 'you'll have your daughter cover'd with a Barbary horse, you'll have your nephews neigh to you; you'll have coursers for cousins, and gennets for germans' (I. i. 113).

Roderigo too is proficient at racist insult, referring to Othello as the 'thick-lips' (I. i. 66) and falling upon the racist stereotype of the lust-ridden black man when he calls to Brabantio that his daughter has given herself to the 'gross clasps of a lascivious Moor' (I. i. 126). Furthermore, the language of these two men ignites a similar tendency to racism lurking within the Brabantio who has in the past invited Othello to his home as guest. Provoked, Brabantio laments in anger that if Desdemona's bewitchment — as he construes it — is to be permitted, then 'Bond-slaves and pagans shall our statesmen be' (I. ii. 99). Othello is of course neither a slave (although, as he tells us, he had once been one) nor a pagan, but Brabantio projects both roles onto the general, referring also to the 'sooty bosom/Of such a thing as thou' (I. ii. 71).

This racism comes, firstly, from two men who are also presented as resentful and envious: the one because he has not been promoted and the other because he is a rejected suitor. Furthermore, their racism makes no impact upon the Venetian court as a whole. Even where Brabantio is concerned, although Iago and Roderigo successfully manage to expose an element of hidden racism, the father's grief is mixed. The problem is as much to come to an understanding of the fact of his daughter's disobedience as it is to cope with his misgivings about his son-in-law's colour. The immense authority which parents claimed during the sixteenth and seventeenth centuries explains at least part of the father's rage. Lawrence Stone provides several vivid illustrations of parent-child relationships at this time:

England was particularly insistent upon the subordination of children to parents, emphasised by outward forms of respect . . . Though he was 63 when he inherited the title in 1666, Sir Dudley North, eldest son of Lord North, 'would never put on his hat or sit down before his father unless enjoined to it'. 'Gentlemen of thirty and forty years old,' recalled Aubrey, 'were to stand like mutes and fools bareheaded before their parents; and the daughters (grown woemen) were to stand at the cupboard-side during the whole time of their proud mother's visit, unless (as the fashion was) leave was desired, forsooth, that a cushion should be given them to kneel upon, brought them by the serving man after they had done sufficient penance in standing.[19]

Moreover, often for the aristocracy and the leading gentry families in England, marriage was parentally advocated and controlled. Property transactions and economic factors were considered too significant to leave entirely to the young people concerned, and although Keith Wrightson detects an increasing flexibility in attitudes he also observes that even whilst change occurred, 'parental domination of match-making may have been stronger in the marriages of daughters than was the case in the matching of sons.'[20] When he is told of his daughter's elopement, Brabantio's first cry is, 'Fathers, from hence trust not your daughters' minds' (I. i. 170) and his insistence that the marriage errs in nature at the very least includes the suggestion that parental loyalty has been flouted. Certainly, Desdemona, when called upon for an explanation, offers one that deals with the issue of parental authority, arguing that she has every right to transfer her duty to her husband:

        My noble father,
I do perceive here a divided duty:
To you I am bound for life and education;

My life and education both do learn me
How to respect you; you are the lord of duty;
I am hitherto your daughter. But here's my husband;
And so much duty as my mother show'd
To you, preferring you before her father,
So much I challenge that I may profess
Due to the Moor, my lord

(I. iii. 189)

Brabantio's final expression of grief communicates anger at deception and betrayal rather than at the 'inter-racial' nature of his daughter's marriage:

Look to her, Moor, if thou hast eyes to see;
She has deceiv'd her father, and may thee.

(I. iii. 293)

The Venetian court ignores the racism implicit or explicit in Brabantio's remarks; they have, after all, elected Othello general and he is, as we learn later in the play, esteemed by them as the 'noble Moor' whom they consider 'all in all sufficient' (IV. i. 265). Certain critics argue that it is only the imminent crisis with the Turks that determines their restraint in the accusation brought against Othello. However, although the emergency clearly dominates their thinking, as would be the case for rulers of any state under threat, no evidence emerges in the detail of the language to suggest that they share a hidden racist disapprobation of Othello. Brabantio's initial accusation, with its racist asides, might well have been taken up by one with racist predilections; instead, the Duke asks only for concrete proof to replace the 'thin habits and poor likelihoods/Of modern seeming' which 'do prefer against him' (I. iii. 109). The first senator attempts, it is true, to ascertain whether Othello did 'by indirect and forced courses/Subdue and poison this young maid's affections' (I. iii. 112), but, even before the evidence has been fully heard, he also acknowledges, in a way that negates any suggestion of racism, that the relationship between Othello and Desdemona might well be based upon 'request, and such fair question/As soul to soul affordeth' (I. iii. 114). When, finally, the truth has been heard, the Duke responds, 'I think this tale would win my daughter too' (I. iii. 171) and his ensuing attempt to console Brabantio — although it obviously suggests, in its platitudinous ring, a desire to move on to the emergency facing Venice — argues for reconciliation and acceptance.[21]

Furthermore, the racism displayed by Iago, Roderigo and, in his uglier moments, Brabantio, contrasts with others in *Othello*. Cassio, the Florentine, clearly loves and respects his general; deprived of office by Othello, he does not resort to the resentment that characterises the response of the ensign who considers he has been passed over. Yearning only to win again his superior's favour, Cassio blames himself:

I will rather sue to be despis'd than to deceive so good a commander with so slight, so drunken, and so indiscreet an officer.

(II. iii. 279)

And Desdemona, also like Iago a Venetian, not only loves Othello but remains consistently in love with him throughout the play, never, despite that to which she is subjected, impugning either that love or her husband.[22]

Nevertheless, at times in the play speakers besides Iago, Roderigo and Brabantio appear to refer to or to draw upon racist discourse. These include the Duke, Desdemona and even Othello himself. Before examining such remarks, and one further attempt by Iago to use racist discourse in an exchange with Othello, we need to consider the overall presentation of Iago and Othello in the text.

3

Winthrop Jordan argues that *Othello* loses most of its power and several of its central points 'if it is read with the assumption that because the black man was the hero English audiences were indifferent to his blackness. Shakespeare was writing both *about* and *to* his countrymen's feelings concerning physical distinctions between peoples . . .'[23] The observation is an important one. Shakespeare is writing about colour prejudice and, further, is working consciously against the colour prejudice reflected in the language of Iago, Roderigo and Brabantio. He in fact reverses the associations attached to the colours white and black that are the consequence of racist stereotyping. It is Iago, the white man, who is portrayed as amoral and anti-Christian, essentially savage towards that which he envies or resents, and cynical in his attitude to love — for him 'merely a lust of the blood and a permission of the will' (I. iii. 335).

Iago's tendencies are exposed to the audience from the start. In reacting to his own failure to secure promotion he attacks both the system that he serves and the man who has won the position he coveted. He voices the time-serving bureaucrat's objection that promotion goes not by the 'old gradation, where each second/Stood heir to th' first' (I. i. 38) and denigrates the abilities of his successful rival as 'Mere prattle, without practice' (I. i. 26). Moreover the viciousness in Iago's seething resentment at having to remain in a condition of subordination, his restless barrack-room malice, flashes out in his cynicism towards Cassio and in his dislike of the alien implicit in his reference to his rival as 'a Florentine' (I. i. 20). Iago's scorn for social bonds or any concept of duty, his assertion, 'not I for love and duty/But seeming so, for my peculiar end' (I. i. 60), identifies his ruthless hypocrisy and self-interest. When he asserts his intention to deceive

> For when my outward action doth demonstrate
> The native act and figure of my heart
> In complement extern, 'tis not long after
> But I will wear my heart upon my sleeve
> For daws to peck at: I am not what I am.
>
> (I. i. 65)

Iago registers his view of the members of his own class as predatory — ready to 'peck at' any exposure of feeling. This negative projection onto his social equals prompts an overtly stated intention to be himself a predator, whilst suppressing all show of private feeling. His picture of the ruling class as ready at the appropriate moment to cashier the 'knee-crooking knave' (I. i. 45) serving it is not borne out by either Cassio's or indeed Othello's experience. Such reactions result patently from a sense of failure and rejection, which, as Jane Adamson observes, he fails to acknowledge:

Iago's significance . . . centres on his unremitting efforts to deny or suppress the feelings that consume him, and to transform them into other feelings that might at once allow and justify a course of retributive action, instead of his having impotently to suffer fear, loss and self disgust, and negation.[24]

Othello is both about love and about its absence. Iago, in rejecting a social conscience and in suppressing all personal emotion, eschews Christian values asserting the importance of a positive and loving commitment to one's fellows and one's society. Moreover, the consequences of Iago's rejection of communication and commitment extend beyond mere escape from the inevitable vulnerability and risk that the action of love to a degree always involves. Iago also loses the capacity to comprehend love. The irony in his racist brooding — especially in his soliloquies about Othello's alleged sexual licence — is that his own mechanistic and cynical view of love (as he outlines it at the conclusion of Act I, and as he claims it for the Venetians), approximates closely to the penchant for lust of which black men were accused in racist accounts. Perhaps nowhere else in drama is Jordan's point about the Elizabethan faculty for *projection* onto the other so well illustrated as in Iago's imaginings about Othello's alleged promiscuity.

On at least two occasions in the text, Iago's amoral and anti-Christian attitude appears to be directly indicated. William Elton has identified an instance of Pelagian heresy in Act I, scene iii:

Virtue? a fig! 'tis in ourselves that we are thus or thus. Our bodies are our gardens, to the which our wills are gardeners; so that if we will plant nettles or sow lettuce, set hyssop and weed up [tine], supply it with one gender of herbs or distract it with many, either to have it sterile with idleness, or manur'd with industry — why the power and corrigible authority of this lies in our wills.   (I. iii. 326)

In extolling man's complete freedom Iago propounds a philosophy which St Augustine laboured to eradicate.[25] Then, when Othello takes his terrible vow (III. iii. 453—62) Iago pledges:

> Witness, you ever-burning lights above,
> You elements that clip us round about,
> Witness that here Iago doth give up
> The execution of his wit, hands, heart,
> To wrong'd Othello's service! Let him command,
> And to obey shall be in me remorse,
> What bloody business ever.

> (III. iii. 469)

The text here echoes Desdemona's earlier language of love to Othello, but, in kneeling and twisting the sentiment into a promise to serve his general in 'what bloody business ever', Iago perverts the first commandment thus desecrating his own morality. In terms of the Christian context of the play, destructiveness emanates from Iago: it is his savagery that, as the play unfolds, tears at the fabric of his society.

In his presentation of Othello as the antithesis of the stereotypical 'Blackamoor', Shakespeare runs counter not merely to Cinthio's treatment of the Moor in *Hecatommithi*, but also to the currents of colour prejudice prevalent in his age. Shakespeare's Othello is invested with the prerequisites of nobility — he is born of 'royal siege' (I. ii. 22), he is a great soldier, he possesses a lofty vision, and Shakespeare gives to him the richest language in the play.[26]

Moreover, as Christian general best suited to defend Cyprus against the Turks, Othello would have had special heroic resonance. As we know, the sixteenth century witnessed a long struggle between Venice and Turkey for control of the Mediterranean — something about which I shall have more to say later. In 1571 the Turks took Famagusta in Cyprus and massacred its inhabitants but in the same year Don Jon managed to defeat the Turkish fleet at Lepanto. According to commentators Lepanto was the battle which turned the tide in favour of the Christian West against the

Ottoman. And repeated battles over Cyprus earlier in the century were a feature of the larger conflict. The prestige attached to Othello's military position by at least part of the Jacobean audience watching the play, should not, therefore, be underestimated.[27]

From a traditional point of view, the nobility of Othello's vision is evident in his capacity for love, and in his concern with justice and honour. Critics often note the richness of his language about love, the 'universal' context it evokes, the awareness of the vulnerability of 'human love' within an unpredictable world, which it also acknowledges. This last point is worth reiterating. For instance, when reunited with Desdemona, Othello says:

> If it were now to die,
> 'Twere now to be most happy; for I fear
> My soul hath her content so absolute
> That not another comfort like to this
> Succeeds in unknown fate.
>
> (II. i. 193)

He expresses not only his joy but recognises an intrinsic part of the love experience. Fear of the vulnerability of love in the context of an uncertain world forms part of Shakespeare's depiction of love again in *Antony and Cleopatra*. During the first act, Cleopatra, confronted by the immediate departure of Antony, at last abandons her anger for an open admission of the immeasurable sense of loss which she fears their parting may produce:

> Sir, you and I must part, but that's not it:
> Sir, you and I have lov'd, but there's not it;
> That you know well, something it is I would, —
> O, my oblivion is a very Antony,
> And I am all forgotten.
>
> (I. iii. 91)[28]

A similar recognition of the unpredictability of the conditions within which human love must express itself accompanies the intensity of Othello's love for Desdemona.

Othello's love is intimately bound up with his sense of honour, and this sense of honour includes the public as well as the private being. The point is sometimes made — perhaps rightly — that present-day attitudes are out of sympathy with a general such as Othello who has so strong a concept of duty to the state. An age which has seen two wars, colonial and post-colonial repression, Vietnam and persisting totalitarian modes of rule, exploitation and warfare — to say nothing of the current role of the South African Defence Force — responds sceptically and suspiciously to military contexts and personalities. But we need to remember that members of the Elizabethan and Jacobean ruling order, at least, did not, presumably, look upon their military heroes with as much scepticism. In any event, as Christian commander of Cyprus, Othello's understanding of marriage does not admit infidelity. And he is not particularly unique in this. Certain commentators in the sixteenth and seventeenth centuries viewed adultery with extreme seriousness. As Stephen Greenblatt observes, it was held to be

one of the most horrible of mortal sins, more detestable, in the words of the *Eruditorium penitentiale,* 'than homicide or plunder', and hence formally deemed punishable, as several authorities remind us, by death. Early Protestantism did not soften this position. Indeed, in the mid-sixteenth century, Tyndale's erstwhile collaborator, George Joye, called for a return to the Old Testament penalty for adulterers. 'God's law' he writes, 'is to punish adultery with death for the tranquillity and commonwealth of His church.' This is not an excessive or vindictive course; on the contrary, 'to take away and to cut off putrified and corrupt members from the whole body lest they poison and destroy the body, is the law of love.' When Christian magistrates leave adultery unpunished, they invite more betrayals and risk the ruin of the realm . . . [29]

The moral laxity at the court of King James, too, perturbed commentators, one of whom wrote of

The holy state of matrimony perfidiously broken and amongst many made but a May game . . . and even great personages prostituting their bodies to the intent to satisfy and consume their substance in lascivious appetites of all sorts. [30]

71

Othello's detestation of adultery sets him amongst the moralists, at the opposite pole from Iago's savage cynicism about sex and love.

Furthermore, Othello's sense of honour is intimately bound up with his belief in justice, evident in the first act not only in the context of his knowledge of the service he has done Venice, which will 'out-tongue' Brabantio's complaints (I. ii. 19), but also in his confidence that the evidence he offers will exonerate him. In Act II he dismisses his own appointee when the evidence convicts him, despite his personal love for Cassio, and in Acts III, IV and V he applies judicial procedures in an attempt to handle the crisis into which he is plunged. His final suicide is also for him an act of justice in which he provides for himself suitable punishment for what he now understands to have been the murder of his own wife.

In his presentation of Othello, Shakespeare appears concerned to separate his hero from the fiction which the racist associations attached to his colour allege. It may be argued that, despite these factors, Shakespeare, in order to make his Moor acceptable, finds it necessary to make him Christian. This is perhaps to notice the obvious — Shakespeare, inevitably, is locked into a particular cultural context. But given this, it is still clear that the thrust in the play is away from the use of the colour black as a negative indicator of human nature. We may recall here, too, that Ernest Jones cites instances from Shakespeare's earlier work to maintain that, although Shakespeare may have begun with unthinking acceptance of the colour prejudice of his age, he started to move beyond this before *Othello*. Whereas the portrayal of Aaron in *Titus Andronicus* largely conforms to the negative Elizabethan racial stereotype, by the time of *The Merchant of Venice* Shakespeare offers a more dignified Moor.[31]

In addition, in *The Merchant of Venice,* which is so concerned with prejudice, Shakespeare appears consciously to register irony during his presentation of Portia's colour prejudice. We may note, in this context, that for the word 'complexion' meaning 'The natural colour, texture, and appearance of the skin esp. of the face', the *Oxford English*

> Mislike me not for my complexion,
> The shadowed livery of the burnish'd sun,
>
> (II. i. 2)[32]

In view of this meaning for the word 'complexion' it is likely that Shakespeare intends us to detect hypocrisy in Portia's polite flattery of the Prince of Morocco's appearance when she tells him that, were he to win,

> Your self . . . then stood as fair
> As any comer I have look'd on yet
> For my affection
>
> (II. i. 22)

when set against her privately stated opinion, upon hearing of the approach of this suitor:

> . . . if he have the condition of a saint and the complexion of a devil, I had rather he should shrive me than wive me.
>
> (I. ii. 125)

and her more overt remark after the Prince's failure to choose the correct casket:

> A gentle riddance, — draw the curtains, go, —
> Let all of his complexion choose me so.
>
> (II. vii. 79)

It is also interesting here to recall that several anti-alien disturbances occurred in England between 1586 and 1596. These involved the presence in the country of Fleming and French workers and their families. Shakespeare is generally believed to be the author of three pages in the play *Sir Thomas More,* which deals with a similar situation and the likely date for which is 1600.[33] More argues, in the lines thought to be by Shakespeare, primarily against the disobedience of the crowd which seeks to riot against the presence of aliens. He shows them 'that their demand for the banishing of foreigners, urged as it is by violence, is a dictation to the government which cannot be allowed.'[34] But the lines also reveal a marked sensitivity and sympathy for the plight of the foreigner under threat:

Graunt them remoued . . .
ymagin that you see the wretched straingers
their babyes at their backs, with their poor lugage
plodding tooth ports and costs for transportacion . . .
. . . by this patterne
not on of you shoold lyve an aged man
for other ruffians as their fancies wrought
with sealf same hand sealf reasons and sealf right
woold shark on you and men lyke revenous fishes
woold feed on on another.
. . . say nowe the king
. . . banysh you, whether woold you go
what country by the nature of your error
shoold gyve you harber go you to Fraunc or Flanders
to any Iarman province, Spane or Portigall
nay any where that not adheres to Ingland
why you must needs be straingers, woold you be pleased
to find a nation of such barbarous temper
that breaking out in hiddious violence
woold not afoord you, an abode on earth
whett their detested knyves against your throtes
spurne you lyke doggs, and lyke as yf that god
owed not nor made not you, nor that the elaments
wer not all appropriat to your comforts
but chartered vnto them, what woold you thinck
to be thus vsed, this is the straingers case
and this your momtanish inhumanyty.[35]

Although these lines apply to European immigrants living in England, they reveal powerful empathy with the plight of outsiders in general.

Perhaps most important is the evidence that G.K. Hunter provides in order to identify a current of writing in the literature of the seventeenth century and earlier which endeavours to abandon the use of the colours black and white as reliable signs of personality and moral fibre. To illustrate this tendency Hunter quotes from Jerome's comment-ary on Ephesians 5:8 ('For ye were sometimes darkness, but now are ye light in the Lord: walk as the children of light') that he 'that committeth sin is of the devil (John 3:8). Born of such a parent first we are black by nature, and even after repentance, until we have climed to Virtue's height . . .' and he cites Bishop Hall, who, encountering a black man, opines:

This is our colour spiritually; yet the eye of our gracious God and Saviour, can see that beauty in us wherewith he is delighted. The true Moses marries a Blackamoor; Christ, his church. It is not for us to regard the skin but the soul. If that be innocent, pure, holy, the blots of an outside cannot set us off from the love of him who hath said, *Behold, thou art fair, my Sister, my Spouse*: if that be foul and black, it is not in the power of an angelical brightness of our hide, to make us other than a loathsome eye-sore to the Almighty.[36]

There is, admittedly, residual racism in such writing: the colour black still attaches to the concept of evil. Nevertheless a separation of the sign black from the essential goodness or evil of human beings also takes place. Such a predilection is suggested too in Shakespeare's reversal, in *Othello,* of the patterns set up by the racist discourse of his age.

4

It is partly in such contexts that we need to consider re-marks made by Desdemona, the Duke and even Othello him-self. In certain lines the characters speak in ways that not only appear to acknowledge the currents of racism in Shake-speare's day but also in ways that play off their actual re-sponses to each other against awareness (which it is impos-sible in terms of literary tradition easily to escape) of current or traditional attachment of (racist) values to these colours as signs. Thus Desdemona speaks of having seen Othello's visage 'in his mind' (I. iii. 252), the Duke tells Brabantio that

> If virtue no delighted beauty lack,
> Your son-in-law is far more fair than black
>> (I. iii. 290)

while Othello himself, in bitterness, is at least partly alluding
to the patristic significance of his colour when he cries out at
what Desdemona's 'adultery' has done to him:

> (Her) name, that was as fresh
> As Dian's visage, is now begrim'd and black
> As mine own face.
>
> (III. iii. 388)

In contrast to these instances, Emilia, torn by grief and anger
at the death of her mistress, cries

> O, the more angel she,
> And you the blacker devil!
>
> (V. ii. 131)

drawing directly upon the racist tendency in patristic and
literary tradition. But earlier, when Emilia asks Desdemona
whether she thinks her husband jealous, Desdemona's reply
suggests an equally direct rejection of this tradition:

> Who, he? I think the sun where he was born
> Drew all such humors from him.
>
> (III. iv. 31)

Desdemona here takes the darkness of her husband's skin as
a positive sign of virtue.

In addition, Othello, as his sense of betrayal intensifies,
intermittently appears to recognise the racism which, present in his world, must lurk at the edges of his consciousness or identity. Iago, aware of this, attempts to penetrate
the integrity of Othello's sense of self and encourage the
general's acceptance of a construction of himself and his inter-
action with others drawn from the discourse of racism. In
Act I Shakespeare presents the love of Othello and Desdemona as extraordinary; the destructive wave that Iago,
exploiting racist impulses, tries to bring against the two, fails.
But in Act III, Iago tries again when he bears witness against
the integrity of Desdemona.[37] After his first warning about
Desdemona (III. iii. 197), and after his deliberate reference to

Venetian 'pranks' that postulates a shared ethical system from which Othello is excluded, he makes a fleeting reference to the possibility of colour prejudice — 'And when she seem'd to shake and fear your looks,/She lov'd them most' (III. iii. 208). Then, a few lines later, as Othello ponders Iago's remark — 'And yet, how nature erring from itself' (III. iii. 227) — Iago takes a direct step into the explosive subject of colour:

> Ay, there's the point; as (to be bold with you)
> Not to affect many proposed matches
> Of her own clime, complexion, and degree,
> Whereto we see in all things nature tends —
> Foh, one may smell in such, a will most rank,
> Foul disproportions, thoughts unnatural.
>
> (III. iii. 233)

Othello's line prompting Iago's interruption may suggest that he entertains, in a fallen world, the prospect of the decline of his and Desdemona's exalted love from its true nature into an adulterous and ordinary plane. However, the line echoes the phrasing of Brabantio's attack upon him at Act I scene iii lines 60—64 and it encourages Iago to intervene with the insinuation of racism. But although Iago works for the substitution of Othello's view of himself by a narrative drawn from racist discourse, he treads on dangerous ground and must, when he goes in the present instance too far, withdraw:

> But (pardon me) I do not in position
> Distinctly speak of her, though I may fear
> Her will, recoiling to her better judgement,
> May fall to match you with her country forms,
> And happily repent.
>
> (III. iii. 238)

The word 'form' in the *Oxford English Dictionary* has as its sense not only 'A body considered in respect to its outward shape and appearance' but also 'manner, method, way, fashion (of doing anything)' (first citation 1297). Elsewhere Iago remains careful to keep his allegations within the bounds of differing social conventions, as when he exploits Othello's position as an outsider to Venetian custom at III. iii. 201—3. Othello himself comments on the fact that he is to an extent a stranger to the intimacies of Venetian social life. Attempting to understand the possible reason for Desdemona's supposed infidelity at another point he refers again to his colour, indicating at once what this signifies for him:

> Haply for I am black,
> And have not those soft parts of conversation
> That chamberers have, or (etc.)
> (III. iii. 265 ; my emphasis)

As soldier as well as 'stranger' Othello is well aware of the difference in behaviour between himself and the 'wealthy curled [darlings]' (I. ii. 68) of whom Brabantio speaks.

Nevertheless, the possibility of, or danger of, racism which Iago, in the exchange at Act III scene iii lines 227—33, attempts to convert into 'fact', occasionally surfaces elsewhere in the language of the Othello who was once a slave. Thus at Act III scene iii line 189 he reflects 'For she had eyes, and chose me.' Endeavouring to dismiss Iago's hints that he might have cause for jealousy, Othello recalls that as suitor he was one of presumably a number of wooers Desdemona might have chosen and sets against an assumed deficiency of merit the fact that Desdemona preferred him. His words, however, give at least partial credence to the racist fictions Iago attempts to encourage, to the possibility that Desdemona herself, incorporates in her 'revolt' an element of racism.

I would argue that such anxiety about the possibility of racism, when it surfaces, remains occasional, inevitably ambiguous and only one fleeting element in the unfolding of Othello's crisis. Some critics, for reasons I will attempt to suggest later in this chapter, ignore the ambiguities in Othello's (infrequent) recognition of the problem and convert an inevitable anxiety about a danger in his world into complete incorporation of racist discourse in his view of himself. In countering this tendency, we should recall too Shakespeare's presentation of Shylock in *The Merchant of*

Venice. The Jew's intense awareness of Christian hostility and aggression never leads him to speak in a way that suggests he has internalised their attitudes in his understanding of himself. Unlike Shylock, Othello is of course admired in Venetian society. But this does not blind him to recognition at times of the threatening and destructive potential in the racist discourse active in his world.

5

Despite Shakespeare's separation of the 'real' Othello from the fiction that racist associations attached to his colour allege, the fact remains that in Act V Othello smothers or strangles his wife. How are we to take this image of violence? Or, to put the question differently, what is the reality that lies behind his action, the appearance of which — in its collocation of violence with a certain colour — has been so inviting to racist interpreters of the play?

The act of desperation presented in the text does not confirm in Othello a special form of 'barbarism' from which, say, certain European peoples are immune, nor, indeed, does the partial corruption of the Othello-language by the Iago-language in Acts IV and V ever include complete acceptance of Iago's racist (as opposed to his socio-cultural) thrust against the general. The murder of Desdemona in traditional terms presents to the audience the most terrible version in the play of the tragedy of human action in its aspect of error. To acknowledge this is to notice those aspects critics have identified in the play which relate to traditional Christian discourse: the concern with the limited faculties of human judgement in a fallen world and the related problem of appearance and reality with which the 'human condition', perceived in this way, has to contend. One of the most strident accusations against Othello has been that he is too gullible, or credible — an 'easy dupe' as Eliot and Leavis would have us believe.[38] The claim is possible only if the critic ignores the concern in *Othello* with the fact that, in such a fallen world, the human being inevitably lacks the divine-like power that would enable him to identify and root out the hidden anti-social and destructive impulses which motivate the actions of certain members of society. Moreover, the play does not trivialise this recognition by proposing that it is the consequence of a particular — and therefore avoidable — susceptibility to weak judgement. Towards the end of the play, Emilia, ironically in the presence of the husband whom the audience knows to be the very 'villainous knave' of whom she complains, yearns for extra-human powers of perception:

> O (heaven), that such companions thou'dst unfold,
> And put in every honest hand a whip
> To lash the rascals naked through the world
> Even from the east to th'west!
>
> (IV. ii. 144)

Such powers, the play continually asseverates, are denied to human beings. The final image of a black man stifling or strangling a white woman, it might be argued, deliberately courts a racist impulse, which we know was likely to have been present in certain members of Shakespeare's first audiences. But it does so only to explode any such response. The play, before this moment, has presented multiple acknowledgements of the different factors which vitiate any hope of perfect perception or judgement in a postparadisial world. I have already noted that colour as surface indicator of identity is shown to be totally inadequate. Again, from the start of the play, in the extended exposure he gives to Iago, together with his presentation of the ensign throughout, Shakespeare concentrates on the problem of the inevitable vulnerability of human judgement to hidden malice. Moreover, in the various 'trial scenes' in the play, Shakespeare demonstrates the extent to which the judicial process itself is subject to abuse because of the unreliability of testimony. These issues underlie the portrayal of Othello's dilemma and they help to register a human problem that is most intensely and painfully presented in that final image of suffocation.

When Shakespeare makes the audience Iago's confidant at the play's beginning, he endows the audience with a position of omniscience that no person outside the theatre can possess — and which the members of the *Othello* world cannot possess either. The audience is invited to realise, accordingly, the danger of concealed anti-social behaviour and, too, its power, for Shakespeare also bestows upon Iago the greatest reputation of anyone in the play for honesty. Paul A. Jorgensen has stressed the frequency with which the word 'honest' is appended to Iago's name and he has also suggested that Iago's official function as ensign may have been to expose knaves.[39] Much literature of the time concerns itself with this problem, explicitly in plays such as *A Knack to Know a Knave* (1594) or in treatises such as 'The Triall of true Friendship; or perfit mirror, whereby to discerne a trustie friend from a flattering Parasite. Otherwise, a knacke, to know a knave from an honest man: By a perfit mirrour of both' (1596).[40] The fact that an honest man cannot be identified by observation was explored in other sixteenth- and seventeenth-century works such as *A Knack to Know an Honest Man* (1596), *Volpone* (1605) and *The White Devil* (c. 1612).

Furthermore, Jorgensen suggests that Iago's 'office' to Othello as ancient and friend 'can be appreciated only if we see in him ... the knave-hunting abilities and profession of the morality Honesty' (p. 14). As a catcher of knaves his reference to Cassio as a 'slipper and subtle knave' (II. i. 242) and his speech remarking 'take mine office' (III. iii. 375) might well have suggested to Jacobean audiences, in addition to an honest man's preoccupation, an official function.[41] Honesty, as Jorgensen points out, can be the best disguise for knavery, and certainly Iago's influence in his society results from his reputation for honesty. He offers himself as a reliable touchstone, ready to speak the truth at whatever cost. His self-interested anti-social impulses, hidden beneath this flawless reputation enable him to take in more effectively, in an ever-widening field of operation not only Roderigo, but also Cassio, Emilia and Desdemona, as well as Othello. In *Macbeth*, Duncan comments on the same difficulty when he says of revealed treachery in that gentleman in whom he had formerly 'built/An absolute trust' (I. iv. 14): 'There's no art/ To find the mind's construction in the face' (I. iv. 12).[42]

Again, the fact that Cassio and Desdemona, as well as Othello, trust Iago cannot be overemphasised. None has the god-like vision — the lack of which Emilia laments — that would enable him or her to penetrate the surface honesty of Iago to discover the reality. Thus Cassio, dismissed from office largely as a result of Iago's skilfully devious manipulation turns nevertheless to the 'honest' ensign for advice. And Desdemona, in her hour of greatest need, which also results from the work of Iago, kneels to the 'honest' friend of her husband to beg for help. Granted the care with which Shakespeare emphasises, in his presentation of Iago, the potency as well as the effectiveness of concealed malice, Othello's only protection against his ensign would be extra-human powers of perception — an X-ray vision granted to no person.

Through his presentation of Iago, Shakespeare demonstrates that in an imperfect world human judgement can never penetrate beyond the opacity of deliberately deceptive discourse. Moreover, Shakespeare explores this problem in the specific context of the process of justice. The narrative fictions a man may weave about himself or others become in the legal context the testimony he offers. And it is most interesting that the vulnerability of testimony to distortion was a particular talking point in the legal discussions of Shakespeare's time and earlier. Amongst other commentators, Robert Boyle, for instance, stressed the crucial role of the witness:

You may consider . . . that whereas it is as justly generally granted, that the better qualified a witness is in the capacity of a witness, the stronger assent his testimony deserves . . . for the two grand requisites of a witness [are] the knowledge he has of the things he delivers, and his faithfulness in truly delivering what he knows.[43]

Barbara Shapiro, who argues that reliance upon testimony was increasing during this period because of the growing mobility and complexity of society, emphasises that the issue was particularly crucial in the matter of witchcraft:

The fact that witchcraft was a crime as well as a phenomenon and thus had to be proved to a learned judge and an unlearned jury . . . provides an unusual opportunity to observe theories of evidence at work. For the courts, witchcraft was a matter of fact and, like all questions of fact, turned on the nature and sources of the testimony . . . [Reginald Scot's *Discoverie of Witchcraft* 1584] exposed one type of trickery and fraud after another and denounced Continental legal procedures which, in cases of witchcraft, permitted excommunicants, infants, and 'infamous' and perjured persons to testify and allowed 'presumption and conjectures' to be taken as 'sufficient proofes.'[44]

In the sixteenth and seventeenth centuries prosecution of witchcraft increased rapidly throughout Europe. Laws against it were passed in 1542 and 1563. Although even more rigorous legislation was enacted in 1604, the probable date of *Othello*, this was not as harsh as that fifty years earlier. Side by side with the legal offensive against witchcraft, the debate about the credibility of witches intensified. In 1616 John Cotta wrote with extreme caution about the use of testimony:

if the witnesses of the manifest magicall and supernaturall act be substantiall, sufficient, able to judge, free from exception of malice, partialitie, distraction, folly, and if by conference and counsell with learned men, religiously and industriously exercised in judging those affairs, there bee justly deemed no deception of sense, mistaking of reason or imagination, I see no true cause, why it should deserve an Ignoramous, or not be reputed a True bill, worthy to be inquired, as a case fit and mature for the same due triall.[45]

The concern with justice in *Othello* clearly relates to these issues. It may be remarked that where doubt about any situation arises the only way in which society may attempt to ascertain the truth after the event is through the process of law. As critics have noted, the series of 'trial' scenes that take place in *Othello* all depend in the main upon testimony. Moreover, the first of these 'trial' scenes centres specifically upon the charge of witchcraft.

Brabantio maintains that Desdemona 'Sans witchcraft' (I. iii. 64) could not have chosen Othello — a fact of which

83

Iago is not slow to remind his general (III. iii. 211). Further-more, Othello himself, during his account of the courtship, explicitly dismisses the charge of witchcraft (I. iii. 169). Othello and Desdemona offer reliable testimony in this scene and the general is 'acquitted'. For those members of Shake-speare's first audiences interested in the law the debate about the judicial process and the complexities associated with reliance upon testimony, in this scene and those that follow, must certainly have been evoked. In the two subsequent 'trial scenes' Iago is chief witness against Cassio and then Desdemona; not only his false testimony but also his oppor-tunist exploitation of various situations prove crucial. Shake-speare emphasises too that the problem posed for the judicial system by the potential unreliability of testimony is not reducible to explanations of extra-human (satanic) propen-sities for evil. Thus Shakespeare lets Iago boast to his audi-ence that his fabrication of evidence or his alert opportunism, which subverts the law, results from the application of intel-lect, partly from what Greenblatt has identified as his talent for 'improvisation' (to which I will return later):

> Thou know'st we work by wit, and not by witchcraft,
> And wit depends on dilatory time.
> Does't not go well?
>
> (II. iii. 374)[46]

The final 'trial scene' in Act V results from the successful abuse of justice which occurs in Acts II and III. The guilty man in that scene is Othello, the one who has cared most about morality and justice during the play. This posits a sceptical and troubled view of the efficacy of the process of justice as an instrument to achieve the ordered identification and administration of the right and the good. The implica-tions about the inadequacy of the judicial system — the sus-ceptibility of legal processes to deception and manipulation — remain at the close of the play.

What is Othello to do when his trusted friend, the Iago who also has an impeccable reputation for honesty in his society, tells him that his wife is an adulteress? Shakespeare presents, in the increasing conflict which Othello experiences after Iago has alleged the adultery of Desdemona, the problem of human perspicacity and its limitations — posed in both the personal and the public or legal contexts in the first two acts — in its most acute form. Committed to love, honour and justice, for Othello as Christian commander of Cyprus, the sanctity of his marriage, the defence of the island, and the maintenance of order are inextricably linked. Just as he will not earlier be seen to neglect his public role because of his private marriage to Desdemona, he cannot prevent the dishonour he imagines to exist in his private life from permeating his whole existence.

This suggests in Othello, as perhaps in Hamlet, in terms of traditional Christian discourse, a heroic aspiration. Hamlet is subject to passion (in the seventeenth-century sense of the word, indicating inner turbulence and imbalance) but he aspires towards consistent action, the traditional values that will achieve justice, towards too, the neo-stoic power of reason he so admires in Horatio.

When Iago suggests to Othello the possibility that he might change, compromise his situation, abandon his commitment to honour, Othello's reaction is fierce:

> Never, Iago. Like to the Pontic Sea,
> Whose icy current and compulsive course
> Nev'r (feels) retiring ebb, but keeps due on
> To the Propontic and the Hellespont,
> Even so my bloody thoughts, with violent pace,
> Shall ne'er look back . . .
>
> (III. iii. 458)

Othello's energy in this speech is already distorted in the direction of destructive violence. However, the imagery he chooses to assert his own commitment to that in which he believes, which now, in the context of the alleged adultery prompts him to thoughts of punishment and revenge, suggests a similar neo-stoic aspiration towards consistency of purpose. Othello sees his commitment to justice and honour (now to be expressed by punitive action) in terms of the great image

85

of the sea and the inevitable sweep of its natural movements. The whole speech from which this extract comes is frightening, but tragically so, partly because the impulses which give rise to the speech are not born of anti-social or destructive motives but of a profound and integrated sense of the importance of human love, honour and justice in both private and public modes of existence.

Othello's most trusted source identifies Desdemona for him as an adulteress. Placed upon the rack he continually struggles against what he cannot at the same time refute without the power of omniscience that Shakespeare has granted only to the audience.

For one thing, he demands evidence: 'Villain, be sure thou prove my love a whore;/Be sure of it. Give me the ocular proof' (III. iii. 360) — evidence which cannot satisfy him because of his love for Desdemona. Iago, we may recall, obliges. After offering him inflammatory images: 'Would you, the [supervisor], grossly gape on?/Behold her topp'd?' (III. iii. 396) he follows with his account of the dream, relying upon the traditional medieval and Renaissance authority of certain dreams as an index to reality. The handkerchief for Othello has similar importance not in itself but because of the vital 'magic' Iago has wrought upon it as a piece of evidence. In the practice of justice such objects are vested with special significance precisely because man is unable to perceive perfectly either past events or present identities. Othello also seeks to communicate with Desdemona directly, but Shakespeare portrays not only how the manipulation of a hidden deceiver may further diminish the normally fallible powers of human perspicacity but also how accidental misunderstanding of the situation affects her powers of judgement so that in her advocacy of Cassio's cause she unwittingly exacerbates the situation and makes Othello's chances of reaching her even more difficult. Similar misconstructions affect the behaviour of Cassio himself and, to a less significant extent, Emilia, Bianca, and Roderigo. Janet Adamson has written instructively on this point, illustrating the extent to which the play shows the many different 'ways and means by which people's thoughts and feelings — whether about others or about themselves — can become fatally tangled, mutually distorting.'[47]

Othello's chance of discovering the truth, we should remember, is further seriously complicated by the theological implications that attach to the theme of appearance and reality. In terms of theology, evil has an almost limitless capacity for concealment, something of which Iago is, indeed, a walking demonstration throughout the play. In *Dr Faustus* Mephistophilis, we may remember, can reappear before Faustus in the semblance of a friar, if he so chooses. Part of the difficulty for Othello is that Desdemona may indeed be the adulteress Iago has claimed she is — and her own behaviour in this is, as I have just remarked, unwittingly provocative. To approach her directly will solve nothing; she will proclaim her 'honesty' with the same apparent integrity that Iago himself displays.

Winifred Nowottny, in what is still one of the most helpful essays on the play, describes the ways in which Act IV offers the 'dreadful spectacle of Othello's attempts to escape' the tension within him between his own image of Desdemona and that which Iago has given him:

The pitch rises as his ways of seeking relief draw, horribly, ever nearer to Desdemona and to the deepest intimacies of love. The falling in a fit is a temporary way of not bearing the tension. That, shocking as it is, affects only himself. The next way is the striking of Desdemona. His striking her in public (for in their private interview there is nothing of this) is a symbolic act: a calling the world's attention to the intolerableness of what he suffers by what he does. The treating Emilia as a brothel-keeper is an expression of the division in him at its deepest level: to go to his wife as to a prostitute is to try to act out what the situation means to him.[48]

The evidence Othello receives continually fails to satisfy him for, as Nowottny also points out, what he wishes to discover is Desdemona's *innocence*. Moreover, the great truth underlying Othello's violence in all this is clear: it has been precipitated not by any innate barbarism of his own but by the barbarism of Iago. The one thing his violence confirms is that if nobility and valour, like depravity and cowardice, are not the monopoly of any colour, then neither is the angry destructiveness that is born of hurt and betrayal. His violence is equalled and often surpassed, as we know, in many of Shakespeare's other plays which have in them only white men.

Othello, Desdemona and Cassio seek only love and honour in the play. The horror of Act V results partly from the fact that, even as Othello kills Desdemona, he still loves her, whilst Desdemona's love, too, remains constant — in dying she blames no one but herself. Othello's language in that final scene, often commented on, shows, side by side with his agonised awareness of the light he is to extinguish, his concern for release, for justice and punishment, his painful, enduring sense of love which ensures that Desdemona, as Christian, be permitted to confess — not merely to confirm her guilt but also to ensure her salvation.

It may be true that *Othello* does acknowledge at its end that anti-social and destructive members of society such as Iago have no more control over their imperfect visions of the world and their actions than anyone else. Iago, despite his attempts at secrecy finds himself exposed. But the justice of his undoing means far less than the errors of those who in the play are good. Their fates result from the danger of language which, because of its opacity, may lend itself to distortion. The inevitable limitations of human judgement, furthermore, make error possible, rendering the good and the just inescapably prey to the actively evil and malign.[49]

6

Although we may examine the play in this way it remains clear that the tragedy is not accounted for, as in *Hamlet*, with the same degree of emphasis upon accident, mystery and a fallen world even if, as we have just seen, this aspect is present in the play. But *Othello* concentrates far more determinedly upon the fact that it is human intervention, the intervention of Iago, that makes the crucial difference. This attention is significant; moreover, the importance of the text's emphasis upon Iago at its commencement extends far beyond the serious play with appearance and reality that is there initiated. The work of recent critics and scholars, to whom the following discussion is especially indebted, has made this abundantly clear.

It is tempting to believe that the choice in *Othello* of the locations Venice and Cyprus is not merely the consequence of the fact that the most likely source of the play, Cinthio's *Hecatommithi,* published in Venice in 1566, so situates the tale of the Moor and Disdemona.[50] Evidence suggests that the Venetian state, and its island Cyprus, would have invited keen, pointed interest from at least the influential and powerful élite in early seventeenth-century audiences watching *Othello.*

Firstly, Venice, a great presence in the Mediterranean in the fifteenth and sixteenth centuries, operated, like Portugal in the Madeira islands, in ways suggesting a colonial power. Cyprus, which the Venetians acquired, was the main Levantine source of sugar; when Portugal through exploitation of virgin soil, slaves and plentiful supplies of wood was able to bring the price of sugar down, the Venetians put their island to use, in addition to the production of sugar, by expanding the production of cotton.[51] By the end of the fifteenth century Venice had no real competitor in supplying cotton to the fustian industry in Europe, and it went on marketing cotton for decades, even after it lost Cyprus to the Turks in 1571.[52]

Secondly, the English audiences that sat down to watch the first performance of *Othello* belonged to a nation that was itself soon to undertake colonisation in the New World. Some Englishmen had argued for and attempted unsuccessfully to initiate such colonisation in the sixteenth century.[53] Despite their failure, and the war with Spain, continuing expansion of trade overseas helped to make future colonisation a possibility. Thus, the Muscovy Company and the commercial explorations of Antony Jenkinson across Russia to Persia contributed to the emergence of a prosperous group of Jacobean merchants and investors with capital and the will to expand.[54] In 1601 the first expedition of the East

India Company set out, to return with a million pounds of pepper and spice and enormous profit for investors.[55] And the Levant Company which operated in the Mediterranean was becoming increasingly important. Moreover its flourishing trade with Turkey coincided with a decline, after 1600, in Venetian domination of the commercial trade between the Orient and Europe and in its shipping, shipbuilding and woollen cloth industries.[56]

When James I made peace with Spain the possibility of trade and expansion in the New World opened up even further.[57] The extent of England's mercantile growth, to say nothing of the examples of Spain and Portugal, encouraged interest in possible colonisation.[58] Those merchants, administrators and investors in Shakespeare's first audiences, we might imagine, aware of the increasing strength of England's thrust into the Mediterranean and toying with ideas of colonisation would have been especially interested in a play presenting the state of Venice (and its island Cyprus) in its heyday.[59] It is useful to add here Immanuel Wallerstein's description of Venice at the height of its power:

In the High Middle Ages, Venice had been the core state of a smaller Mediterranean regional economy, a prefiguration of the European world-economy. Not only was it a centre of trade, of finance and of textile production but it had an imperium stretching down the Adriatic (Dalmatia) to the Aegean. Crete and Cyprus played the same role *vis à vis* Venice that the West Indies would later play *vis à vis* first Spain, then England. They were centres of sugar estates farmed by slaves, as well as slave marts for the surrounding region. The slaves were primarily Slavs and Tartars from the Balkans and the Black Sea, not Black Africans, but the social system was the same . . . Venice was a thriving metropolis where the wealthier merchant classes controlled the state and the intermediate skilled workers were effectively 'unionised' via the guild system. The underclasses were of non-Venetian origin.[60]

Even in the first decades of the seventeenth century, despite the profound factors that were producing its inevitable decline, Venice 'seemed to shine very brightly . . . [although] it was glitter and façade by then' (p. 44). Conversely, as

Wallerstein points out, England, which had in the late Middle Ages been a colony of Europe, an exporter of raw materials (wool) for continental manufacturers, itself underwent, as the sixteenth century unfolded, a transition from a colonial to a core state.[61] In terms of Wallerstein's account, too, the Venice-Cyprus conjunction might have offered more than simply the allure of the exotic to many in the early seventeenth-century English audience.

Other factors also invite recognition that *Othello* in part suggests, draws upon and contributes to the discourse of colonialism. If English colonisation of the New World had, in most senses, yet to commence at the beginning of the seventeenth century, this was not the case within the British Isles. There, commentators observe, a process akin to colonisation was under way in Wales and, especially, in Ireland.[62] British penetration into Ireland had been going on since the 1530s and it sought

to consolidate and expand British political control and economic exploitation of a strategic marginal area previously only partially under British authority. D.B. Quinn has shown that the major policies of this expansion included plantation of British settlements in key areas, the establishment of a docile landed élite, the fossilisation of the social order in areas under British control . . . and the introduction of English as the sole official language (p. 55).

In the context of these developments we may recognise the inevitable emergence of a discourse of colonialism. It seems likely that this received impetus too from the encounters of explorers and adventurers in Africa, and the growth of travel writing to which I referred at the beginning of this chapter.[63] We may recall also Jordan's arguments about the English reaction to the people of Africa.[64] And, as I have earlier indicated, the English were certainly aware of the practice of slavery amongst other nations before engaging in it themselves later in the seventeenth century.

Paul Brown's account of masterlessness and savagism helps us to turn to certain aspects of the discourse of colonialism especially interesting for *Othello:*

91

Masterlessness analyses wandering or unfixed and unsupervised elements located in the internal margins of civil society ... Savagism probes and categorises alien cultures on the external margins of expanding civil power ... At the same time as they serve to define the other, such discursive practices refer back to those conditions which constitute civility itself. Masterlessness reveals the mastered (submissive, observed, supervised, deferential) and masterful (powerful, observing, supervising, teleological) nature of civil society. Savagism (a-sociality and untrammelled libidinality) reveals the necessity of psychic and institutional order and direction in the civil regime. In practice these two concepts are intertwined and mutually reinforcing.[65]

The dominant order in the metropolis, which regards itself and the existing relationships of domination and subordination of which it is part as the embodiment of civility, sends its functionaries to operate the colonial apparatus at the periphery.[66] There, its representatives, in turn, stand for civility and assert mastery over the population subordinated to the colonial power, contesting the masterlessness and savagism that in one way or another challenges that mastery.

Othello's role as Christian commander of Cyprus may be partly apprehended in the context of such discourse, itself suggested by the various ways in which England undertook Irish colonisation, dreamed intermittently of directing its mercantile growth into colonisation of the new world, or encountered Africa. Othello represents the masterful civil society which must deal both with the submissive Cypriot population and with the alien Turkish power (and culture) which threatens the periphery of Venetian dominance. His reaction whilst still in Venice, to the play's first presentation of civil disorder:

> Keep up your bright swords, for the dew will rust them.
> Good signior, you shall more command with years
> Than with your weapons.

> (I. ii. 61)

reflects not only martial and military confidence but shows how this is allied to notions of decorum and faith in the dominant class's capacity to dispense justice (a faith which

92

by the end of the first act appears justified). He also assures the principals of Venetian power that Desdemona's presence in Cyprus will not impede in any way his ability to administer that power. This has been frequently misread as an indication of Othello's sexual limitations; in fact his commitment to an absolute respect for civility is presented as a deliberate contrast to Iago's already much bruited — to the audience — self-interest and cynicism about the dominant order he serves.

Othello's sense of his position as representative of a colonial power that must maintain civility is evident not only in his attitude towards sexual pleasure as being potentially subversive, but also in his response, on Cyprus itself, to the potential threat which disorder — attendant upon the quarrel which Iago has stage-managed — poses:

> Are we turn'd Turks, and to ourselves do that
> Which heaven hath forbid the Ottomites?
> For Christian shame, put by this barbarous brawl.
> He that stirs next to carve for his own rage
> Holds his soul light; he dies upon his motion.
> Silence that dreadful bell, it frights the isle
> From her propriety.
>
> (II. iii. 176)

Recognising Montano's gravity and stillness, and upbraiding him 'that you unlace your reputation thus' (II. iii. 194) Othello turns with angry concern to the effect that this brawling amongst the military apparatus of the dominant colonial class will have upon the subordinate classes of the island:

> What, in a town of war,
> Yet wild, the people's hearts brimful of fear,
> To manage private and domestic quarrel?
> In night, and on the court and guard of safety?
> 'Tis monstrous.
>
> (II. iii. 217)

Behind this language lies the colonial ruler's fear of disorder; it suggests the ruling class's reaction to that 'other' which is:

a threat around which the governing classes might mobilise, that is, around which they might recognise their common class position, as governors, over and against the otherwise ungoverned and dangerous multitudes.[67]

The 'other' becomes feared as barbarous and disruptive, requiring order and civility.

This fear of the 'other' operated in the metropolis as well as on the periphery. As I have briefly indicated in the chapter on *Hamlet* recent critical work has made only too clear the extent to which the Tudor and Stuart monarchies were not absolute in power, and the extent to which we need to set, against the ideologies of hierarchy, the actual political, social and economic history of the age. Fear of difference, of rebellion, of the unmanageable in political and administrative contexts produced in the ruling class a need to define that 'other' against which the norms of its own civility could be continually measured. Thus Paul Brown describes the

socially specific production of the 'masterless man', the ungoverned and unsupervised man without the restraining resources of social organisation, an embodiment of directionless and indiscriminate desire. Masterless types were discerned in royal proclamations to exist in the very suburbs of the capital ... The discourse of masterlessness was embodied also in proclamations and statutes requiring that the bodies of vagrant classes, for example, should be modified. Those condemned as persistent vagrants could be literally marked (whipped, bored, branded) with public signs announcing their adulteration, the hallmark of vice. Alternatively they could suffer the discipline of the work-house or the Bridewell. Yet no apparatus seemed sufficient to keep their numbers down. The constant vilification and punishment of those designated masterless by the ruling classes was not simply a strategy designed to legitimate civil rule: it also evidences a genuine anxiety. This took several forms: a real fear of the governed classes should they mobilise against their betters; a complex displacement of the fear of aristocratic revolt onto the already vilified (p. 52, p. 54).

This fear of the 'other' and the way it may be dealt with by the dominant class, within the metropolitan social order as well as at the periphery, in terms of the masterlessness or savagism it endeavours to dominate, manifests itself in *Othello*, not only

in Act II but at the end of the play. There Othello is brought
to the recognition that as ruler who should embody civility
he has, through his mistake, enacted a disordered justice that
is in fact murder. Moreover the disruptive impulses at work
have come partly from within himself. After reaffirming his
sense of his identity in his past loyalty and service to the
state, his past role as military and administrative representative of civility, he applies to himself the image of the 'other',
that which lies beyond what constitutes civility. It is as
infidel that he punishes those impulses within himself which
have produced disruption:

> Set you down this;
> And say besides, that in Aleppo once,
> Where a malignant and a turban'd Turk
> Beat a Venetian and traduc'd the state,
> I took by th' throat the circumcised dog,
> And smote him — thus.
>
> (V. ii. 356)

Othello's attitudes in the final act reflect the position he
holds as devoted servant as well as member of the dominant
class, as military and colonial administrator on the periphery
of the state's power. He is earlier in the play revered and
respected by the Venetians precisely because he so ably represents and defends their interests. In the case of any agent
of the dominant class, it might be observed, such able service
depends in part upon the perpetuation of certain myths —
amongst them, as we have just seen, the displacement of profoundly based fears of disorder or internal dissension onto
the 'other'.[68] The journey Othello takes in the play, however, leads him by its end to the discovery that his own class
and being are constituted not merely in the mastery of civility
but in antagonisms, conflict, contradiction as well. Moreover
his error itself demonstrates, for the audience, the potential
within the dominant order, or its representatives in the
colonial apparatus on the periphery, for malfunction and
violence. But this recognition is more fully and more alarmingly made in the presentation of Iago.

Despite the temptation to pursue this kind of reading, the

text establishes certain limits beyond which it seems unwise to go. Thus it is clear that, apart from the reference Othello makes in Act II to the subordinate order on Cyprus, the 'colonised' are almost completely absent. This is similar to the presentation of the majority of the population not only in *Hamlet*, but in most of Shakespeare's plays. With the slight exception of *King Lear* and certain elements in *Measure for Measure*, the masses seem to be marginalised as much as possible, certainly in the plays likely to have been written in the period 1601—06.

If the location of Venice and Cyprus — and what this together with other factors suggests — invites a reading that takes the discourse of colonialism into account, it must be emphasised, nevertheless, that the play remains mainly concerned, not with the relationship between coloniser and colonised but with the internal workings of the ruling class itself. This is presented firstly within the relative safety of metropolitan Venice, where the justice of the governing class is seen to work successfully in containing possible disruption. The play then shifts to the more vulnerable and exposed periphery of Cyprus. Here the operation of the colonial apparatus, in the absence of the principals of Venetian power, proves subject to inner dissension, disruption and self-destruction.

Of anyone in the play Iago offers the most striking example of untrammelled libidinousness and a-sociality which the discourse of colonialism defines as the marks of savagism. As we have seen, his much discussed cynicism about love and sex, his libidinous imagination, language and suggestions about the sexual behaviour of those around him, and his tendency to project these fevered impulses onto Othello, all contrast starkly with Othello's capacity for love, his Christian sense of marriage, his hatred of adultery. I have already noted too, how Iago's secret a-sociality is identified at the start of the play, but we need to return to this for a moment here. Himself a member of the dominant colonial order, Iago makes his own attitude to service — the opposite of that expressed in Othello's language and behaviour — clear:

> You shall mark
> Many a duteous and knee-crooking knave
> That (doting on his own obsequious bondage)
> Wears out his time, much like his master's ass,
> For nought but provender, and when he's old, cashier'd.
>
> (I. i. 48)

Iago argues that the exploitative and dominant master hides the real character of his dominance over the servant behind concepts of duty and loyalty. His view in effect asserts that service and mastery will always entail exploitation. Moreover, he determines upon engineering the subversion of his master's position by enacting the very principle he has identified as being operative in the ruling class's legitimation of service. As we have already observed he hides his thrust to dominate Othello by presenting the relationship under the aegis of 'honesty' and under alleged adherence to traditional doctrines about loyal service (which are nevertheless used, in his estimation, to conceal an exploitative relationship). What is especially important for the present discussion is the fact that these secret views in no way prove a hindrance to Iago's retention of his position within the military and colonial apparatus. On the contrary, for almost the entire length of the play — certainly for the period during which the disruption he promotes has almost completely enacted itself — they prove effective. The kind of service Othello offers the dominant class, by contrast, emerges as vulnerable and weak when placed against the attack of another servant within that class such as Iago.

Stephen Greenblatt has described the skill which Iago displays, not merely in hiding his motives but in using language in order to manipulate and redirect the behaviour of others, or his skill in taking advantage of the opportune and unprepared-for moment, as characteristic of a Renaissance tendency, which he calls improvisation.[69] It is necessary to examine Greenblatt's argument in some detail here. He suggests that amongst Iago's skills are to be found 'a sharp eye for the surfaces of social existence . . . a reductive grasp of human possibilities.' He is 'sensitive to habitual and self-limiting forms of discourse', and 'demonically sensitive to the way individuals interpret discourse, to the signals they ignore and those to which they respond' (pp. 234–5). To illustrate other Renaissance instances of this art of improvisation, Greenblatt recounts a story told by Peter Martyr, in 1525, about certain Spanish raids upon islands in the Lucayas (now called the Bahamas) in order to replete a serious labour shortage which the Spaniards were encountering in their gold mines:

Two ships reached an outlying island . . . where they were received with awe and trust. The Spanish learned through their interpreters that the natives believed that after death their souls were first purged of their sins in icy northern mountains . . . then borne to a paradisial island in the south, whose beneficent, lame prince offered them innumerable pleasures: 'the souls enjoy eternal delights, among the dancings and songs of young maidens, and among the embracements of their children, and whatsoever they loved heretofore . . .' When the Spanish understood these imaginations, writes Martyr, they proceeded to persuade the natives 'that they came from those places, where they should see their parents, and children, and all their kindred and friends that were dead: and should enjoy all kind of delights, together with the embracements and fruition of beloved things.' Thus deceived, the entire population of the island passed 'singing and rejoicing,' Martyr says, onto the ships and were taken to the gold mines of Hispaniola (p. 226).

Greenblatt argues that this skill of improvisation displays

the ability both to capitalize on the unforeseen and to transform given material into one's own scenario . . . what is essential is the Europeans' ability again and again to insinuate themselves into the pre-existing political, religious, even psychic structures of the natives and to turn those structures to their advantage (p. 227).

And, finally, he suggests that such improvisation depends upon:

the ability and willingness to play a role, to transform oneself, if only for a brief period and with mental reservations, into another. This necessitates the acceptance of disguise, the ability to effect a divorce, in Ascham's phrase, between the tongue and the heart. Such role-play-

98

ing in turn depends upon the transformation of another's reality into a manipulable fiction (p. 228).

In *Othello,* however, Iago, unlike the Spaniards, turns these skills against members of his own class — this includes Roderigo, Emilia, Cassio and Desdemona, as well as Othello. Greenblatt suggests he is able to do this, firstly, because of the general submission of the characters in *Othello* to *narrativity.* They perceive themselves in terms of narrative, as in the tale Othello offers about his past and as in Desdemona's response to that tale.[70] Iago 'knows that an identity that has been fashioned as a story can be unfashioned, refashioned, inscribed anew in a different narrative' (p. 238). Moreover, and this is perhaps for the present discussion the most significant point in Greenblatt's argument, Iago is able to play on Othello's 'buried perception of his own sexual relations with Desdemona as adulterous' (p. 233). This is possible not because of the position Othello holds nor because of his 'Moorish' past. It is possible primarily because of that in Othello which connects with 'the centuries-old Christian doctrine of sexuality, policed socially and psychically . . . by confession' (p. 246):

Christian orthodoxy in both Catholic and Protestant Europe could envision a fervent mutual love between husband and wife, the love expressed most profoundly by St Paul . . . but like the Pauline text . . . all such discussions of married love begin and end by affirming the larger order of authority and submission within which marriage takes its rightful place (p. 241).

Desdemona's submission to Othello is total and it implies a deeply erotic response to him. This, suggests Greenblatt, has in turn a violent and unsettling effect upon Othello because, even as it prompts mutual thriving in love, it incites what is also considered to be the vice of bad blood.[71] Both Catholic and Protestant writing condemned excess in marital love as akin to adultery. As I suggested earlier, Iago's own fevered projections of adultery onto Othello, and his attitude to sexual behaviour reflects ultimately a similar impulse to demonise sexual desire, to punish it, to displace it onto the 'other'. His cynicism does not free him from these impulses; it is precisely his understanding of the fear of these impulses that enables him to gain entry into Othello's narrative fashioning of Desdemona.

We may recall here the way in which Iago first attempts to attack Othello by exploiting the facts of Othello's past in slavery and that which still makes him partly a stranger in Venice. With such facts the text almost deliberately highlights a surface ambiguity in Othello which suggests points of connection with the 'other', with that which lies beyond the domain of civility. These superficial points of connection encouraged the emergence, in the nineteenth century especially, of the view of Othello as 'erring barbarian' and gave rise to the — in my opinion — racist tradition of criticism, popularised in the twentieth century by writers such as Eliot, Leavis and Lerner to which I will turn in a moment. But the text itself, situating Othello within the dominant class, not beyond it, also invests Othello with attributes which make him, of that class, an exemplar.

Iago's early attempts to re-align Othello by means of those facts connecting him to the 'other', and the racist innuendo he draws upon to suggest them, prove impotent (although, as we have seen, once Othello's equilibrium has been disturbed he attempts, by referring to Venetian custom for instance, to exploit these factors once more). When these attempts to exploit Othello's strangeness fail, Iago turns to the Christian doctrine of sexuality — that which not only connects Othello to the dominant order he serves but which also lies at the centre of that order's culture. In other words, he abandons the attempt to locate disorder in Othello himself, and finds it instead in Othello's bed, in Desdemona. Greenblatt observes that

like the Lucayan religion to the conquistadors, the orthodox doctrine that governs Othello's sexual attitudes — his simultaneous idealization and mistrust of women — seems to Iago sufficiently close to be recognizable, sufficiently distant to be manipulable (p. 246).

It is, however, important to stress that the orthodox doctrine which enables Iago to gain entry into Othello's narrative fashioning is not Lucayan, but Christian. And the complex attitudes which relate to sexuality that Greenblatt describes are ones that would have operated in profound ways for the Jacobean audience, which shared Othello's religion, too. Through his exploitation of these complexities within the culture of the dominant class, Iago is able to reverse the process of displacement. He recalls the displaced and demonised desire that has been lodged in the libidinous and uncontrollable 'other', and he redirects it into Desdemona. Iago knows that this discovery of disorder within his class and within his marriage will prompt in the commander, who must represent civility and who is throughout the play in commitment demonstrably Christian, the impulse to punish and to eradicate. All the more so because the suggestion of illegitimate sexuality parallels, as it must for all intense relationships within this culture, that desire within Othello's own breast. Such desires, as Greenblatt shows, inevitable in any deeply felt erotic relationship, suggest deep rooted complexities within this culture, because they are at the same time defined within Christian discourse as themselves adulterous. If Othello had even remotely within him the marks of savagism he would not be as vulnerable as Iago finds he is.

The doctrines of civility, order and hierarchy used by the dominant colonising order to legitimate its hegemony, allege unity within that order and within its agents. In *Othello* the range of disturbing ambiguities that emerge from events on Cyprus points to the text's unease about this claim. If Othello's very connection with the culture of which he is himself one of the potent representatives renders him vulnerable, the ambiguities in the behaviour of Iago are even more disturbing. His mode of utterance and his manipulation of judicial procedures in Acts II and III, together with his own cynicism both about the internal workings of the civil administrative apparatus, and about its experience of sexuality, offer, throughout the play, clear demonstration of the extent to which agents of the dominant class may actually operate. They may do so in ways totally disconnected from those traditional values often used to legitimate the dominant order's hegemony, or its operation on the periphery. And

Iago's skill with improvisation has specific implications which reflect invidiously upon existent judicial procedures available within the social order. State power claims to enact its authority partly through such judicial procedures which, it asserts, enables those values of justice deriving from traditional Christian discourse to prevail.

Disturbing ambiguity is, furthermore, evident in the deadly antagonisms within the whole military/colonial apparatus that are revealed as the play unfolds. As I have already remarked, in the first act the attack upon Othello made secretly by those who serve him is resolved in the presence of the ruler, but from Act II on the ruler is absent from ensuing events.[72] In the absence of the ruler the military/colonial apparatus on Cyprus proves subject to internal division, antagonism, and violence. The disruptive savagism that in terms of the discourse of colonialism should reside in the 'other' and provide for the governing class a unifying factor confirming a civility that radiates psychic and institutional order is shown instead, in multiple ways, to reside within that dominant class. Moreover the text's inversion of stereotypes enables it to present as most disruptive that agent of the dominant class who looks least like the alien colonised classes within whom savagism is supposed to reside.

Such unease seems implicitly to reflect upon the real nature of that government of civility that was through its agents asserting its mastery in Ireland and dreaming, at least, of asserting it elsewhere. Side by side with this recognition and its unease, we may, finally, set Greenblatt's remarkable passage describing Spenser, one of the masters, as he calls him, of English civility:

in art and in life, his conception of identity ... is wedded to his conception of power, and after 1580, of colonial power. For all Spenser's claims of relation to the noble Spencers of Wormleighton and Althorp, he remains a 'poor boy', as he is designated in the Merchant Taylor's school and at Cambridge, until Ireland. It is there that he is fashioned a gentleman, there that he is transformed from the former denizen of East Smithfield to the 'undertaker' — the grim pun unintended but profoundly appropriate — of 3 028 acres of Munster land

... For what services, we ask, was Spenser being rewarded? And we answer blandly, for being a colonial administrator. But the answer, which implies pushing papers in a Dublin office through endless days of tedium is an evasion. Spenser's own account presses in upon us the fact that he was involved intimately, on an almost daily basis, throughout the island, in the destruction of the Hiberno-Norman civilisation, the exercise of a brutal force that had few if any of the romantic trappings with which Elizabeth contrived to soften it at home. Here, on the periphery, Spenser was an agent of and an apologist for massacre, the burning of mean hovels, and of crops with the deliberate intention of starving the inhabitants, forced relocation of peoples, the manipulation of treason charges so as to facilitate the seizure of lands, the endless repetition of acts of military 'justice' calculated to intimidate and break the spirit ... Ireland is not only in book 5 of *The Faerie Queen*; it pervades the poem. Civility is won through the exercise of violence over what is deemed barbarous and evil, and the passages of love and leisure are not moments set apart from this process but its rewards.[73]

In the two plays Shakespeare seems most likely to have turned to after *Othello,* we may detect this unease about the workings of power, even more intensely pursued, but moved back again from the periphery to the metropolis.

7

Although *Othello* is often taught at tertiary level, South African critics have been wary of writing about the play. When they have done so they hardly touch upon its concern with colour and seek refuge instead in a focus upon idealist abstractions or upon interiority. Thus one critic sees the play as a 'tragedy of love overcome by cynicism'. Othello, only briefly referred to in this article, has a 'magic' love whereas Desdemona's love is superior, suggesting something 'more mature, a human grace humanly worn not supernatural' and she manifests throughout the play 'integrity' and 'higher possession of self'.[74]   Another critic, to whom I have already referred in chapter 1, 'Shakespeare Depoliticised', stresses the play's concern to reveal essential insights into 'human nature'.[75] I would argue that in the South African situation, such preoccupation with the essence of love itself (with

103

Othello inevitably coming out second best), or with the 'truths' of human nature, encourages, through a process of omission and avoidance, docility and continuing submission to the prevailing social order. It is important to recognise, too, that this practice in South African criticism (or teaching) of the play offers, inevitably, a narrow and attenuated version of certain European and American perspectives. Moreover, in these approaches as well, dangerous ambiguities may be detected which perhaps ought not to be fleetingly noted in passing but more directly addressed. We may recall here the observation of Charles Husband, the social psychologist, that 'it is the deterministic association of category of person with type of behaviour that is at the core of race thinking':

racism refers to a system of beliefs held by the members of one group which serve to identify and set apart the members of another group who are assigned to a 'race' category on the basis of some biological or other invariable, 'natural seeming', characteristic which they are believed to possess, membership of this category then being sufficient to attribute other fixed characteristics to all assigned to it.[76]

Such approaches tend to ignore the play's concern with the tragic problems attendant upon human judgement and perception. They choose instead to focus, often obsessively, upon Othello himself. Whilst Bradleyan notions encourage this tendency, it is difficult in most cases to avoid the conclusion that the attribution to Othello of certain characteristics on the basis of his colour, provides the springboard for the ensuing interpretations.

Students with no more than a fleeting encounter with the critical writing on *Othello* will know that, within the framework of traditional Anglo-European approaches, there have been, until recently at least, two ways of regarding the play's hero. The one may be summarised by the title which Helen Gardner's well-known article on the play bears, 'The Noble Moor'. [77] The other has as one of its famous adherents T.S. Eliot, who asserted that he had 'never read a more terrible exposure of human weakness . . . than the last great speech of Othello' where the hero could be seen to be 'cheering himself up' and 'endeavouring to escape reality'.[78] Eliot's strictures added to a body of criticism which then and since then has always included, at various moments, a series of highly personal attacks upon the *adequacy* as well as the general characteristics of Othello's nature. It is the racist aspect of this second highly censorious view that I wish to discuss here.

F.R.Leavis's somewhat notorious essay on *Othello* provides an example.[79] In the course of presenting his case against Bradley's view of Othello as a 'nearly faultless hero whose strength and virtue are turned against him' (p. 137), Leavis lets slip some singular observations. For instance, discussing Othello's marriage to Desdemona he comments that 'his colour, *whether or not* "colour-feeling" existed among the Elizabethans, *we are certainly to take* as emphasizing the *disparity* of the match' (p. 142; my emphasis). This insistence on Othello's blackness as a sign of the 'disparity' in the marriage is accompanied later by another, at best ambiguous, remark that, under Iago's pressure, 'Othello's inner timbers begin to part at once, *the stuff of which he is made begins at once to deteriorate and show itself unfit*' (p. 144; my emphasis). Moreover, despite his apparently sarcastic reference to Othello's relatively mature age when he writes of the 'trials facing him now that he has married this Venetian girl with whom he's "in love" so imaginatively (we're told) as to outdo Romeo and who is so many years younger than himself' (p. 142), Leavis still manages, later in the argument, to find Othello guilty of 'self-centred and self-regarding satisfactions — pride, sensual possessiveness, appetite', and 'strong sensuality with ugly vindictive jealousy'. These defects are then compounded with a series of other telling weaknesses: 'an obtuse and brutal egotism', 'ferocious stupidity' and an 'insane and self-deceiving passion' (pp. 145—7). Leavis develops Eliot's accusation that Othello lacks insight, in a somewhat tortuous observation that links up no doubt (for Leavis) with the 'unfitness' of his Moor's 'inner timbers' when he concludes that Othello's last speech 'conveys something like the full complexity of Othello's *simple nature*'

(p. 151; my emphasis).

Small wonder perhaps that Sir Laurence Olivier's *tour de force* in the National Theatre's production of *Othello* during the mid-1960s (subsequently filmed) disappointed some — despite its disturbing popular appeal. The programme notes accompanying the performance of the play offered liberal extracts from Leavis's essay, perpetuating the notion, already prevalent in Shakespeare's day, of the black man as savage, as sensual and vindictively jealous, and also of course, as simple.[80]

To notice such peccant ambiguities (at best) in Leavis's writing is not to offer a gratuitous slur. Apart from the fact that the subject matter of *Othello* demands that we recognise the question of colour, and the possibility of prejudice, this mode of regarding Othello stretches far back in English criticism. Thomas Rymer, one of the most famous of the play's detractors is best known for his censure: 'So much ado, so much stress, so much passion and repetition about an Handkerchief! Why was not this call'd the *Tragedy of the Handkerchief?*'[81] But the quality of his criticism is perhaps better represented by another of his adjurations deserving as widespread notoriety: 'this may be a caution to all Maidens of Quality how, without their Parent's consent, they run away with *Blackamoors*' (quoted in Vickers, p. 27).

No less a commentator than Coleridge had this to say:

it would be something monstrous to conceive this beautiful Venetian girl falling in love with a veritable negro. It would argue a disproportionateness a want of balance in Desdemona, which Shakespeare does not appear to have in the least contemplated.[82]

Coleridge also shares a tendency noticeable in nineteenth-century criticism to make Othello an Arab rather than an African.[83] And A.C. Bradley, writing at the beginning of the twentieth century reflects as follows on Othello's colour:

Perhaps if we saw Othello coal-black with the bodily eye, the aversion of our blood, an aversion which comes as near to being merely physical as anything human can, would overpower our imagination and sink us below not Shakespeare only but the audiences of the seventeenth and eighteenth centuries.[84]

Even more shocking than the presence of such notions in the minds of earlier critics writing about the play, is the fact that they appear to be shared by one of the most influential of the relatively recent editors of *Othello*. Tellingly, the New Arden edition is still repeatedly set for the use of South African students. Its introduction contributes to the particular strain of racism which accompanies so much of English writing about the play. M.I. Ridley, the editor, appears at one point to dismiss a typical nineteenth-century racist response manifest in the ruminations of a lady 'from Maryland' quoted also in the New Variorum edition of *Othello*. But a passage from Ridley's purported dismissal of her comments is enough to indicate the flavour of his own attitudes. He takes the lady to task in the following way:

Now a good deal of trouble arises, I think, from a confusion of colour and contour. To a great many people the word 'negro' suggests at once the picture of what they would call a 'nigger', the woolly hair, thick lips, round skull, blunt features, and burnt-cork blackness of the traditional nigger minstrel. Their subconscious generalization is . . . silly . . . There are more races than one in Africa, and that a man is black in colour is no reason why he should, even to European eyes, look sub-human. One of the finest heads I have ever seen on any human being was that of a negro conductor on an American Pullman car. He had lips slightly thicker than an ordinary European's, and he had somewhat curly hair; for the rest he had a long head, a magnificent forehead, a keenly chiselled nose, rather sunken cheeks, and his expression was grave, dignified, and a trifle melancholy. He was coal-black, but he might have sat to a sculptor for a statue of Caesar, or, so far as appearance went, have played a superb Othello.[85]

The lingering preference for the Ridley text in South African universities is unlikely to be purely coincidental. Interestingly, however, at secondary level, where South African students are exposed to little more than the text itself, *Othello* is rarely taught. The South African educative authorities clearly sense something in the play itself sufficiently inimical to

107

racist ideology and practice to discourage its use in high schools.

More recently than Ridley, Laurence Lerner, in arguing that we should not 'sentimentalise' Othello, participates in the tradition of criticism developed by Eliot and Leavis. [86] We may be certain that, as an ex-South African, Professor Lerner eschews racism of any kind and his article presumably attempts to avoid not merely overt racism but also the covert inverted racism that might be detected in an unsubstantiated over-eager defence of Othello. But having respectfully quoted both Eliot and Leavis, he cannot, whatever we may wish to speculate about his motives, for long remain on the sidelines. Lerner presents Othello as an amalgam of the noble and the jealous, the soldier and the fool, the Christian and the barbarian who is reduced to 'stammering bestiality' in the course of the play (p. 352). There is, however, no need to linger over the intermittent ambiguous comments that punctuate his article for its true tenor becomes clear towards the end:

Othello is a convert. Noble and upright as he is, he seems all the nobler *when you consider what he was* — a Negro [sic] a barbarian [sic] . . . Everyone remarks in the first act that Othello is black, that the environment he grew up in is one where passions rule . . . when Othello falls there comes to the surface just this black savage that everyone in the first Act was so pleased that he wasn't . . . I am afraid Shakespeare suffered from colour prejudice. *Othello* is seldom played in South Africa, where it is not thought proper for white women to marry black men. I am never sure that the South Africans are wise about this: for if one can put aside the hysterical reaction that any play depicting inter-marriage must be wicked, one should be able to see quite a lot of the South African attitude present (pp. 357—60; my emphasis).

Othello as a public relations exercise for apartheid!

Equally distressing in much critical writing about the play is the fact that certain associations attached to the colours black and white in literary and iconographic tradition appear to have remained embedded in and affected the attitudes of twentieth-century critics towards the dramatic characters in *Othello*. Lerner provides a clear instance of this with his observation:

Blackness is the symbol, in the imagery, not only for evil but for going beyond the bounds of civilisation: in the end, the primitive breaks out again in Othello. The two Othellos are one: the play is the story of a barbarian who (the pity of it) relapses (p. 360).

The dangerous insistence on blackness as the 'heart of darkness', so pressingly present too in Conrad's famous story — blackness as strongly linked with the primitive, the savage, the simple — lurks within many ostensibly non-racist articles as well.[87] Thus, in a well-meaning article which is nevertheless of this kind, K.W. Evans is unable to shake off racist overtones in his use of the terms 'blackness' and 'whiteness'.[88] He observes:

Othello's blackness, the primary datum of the play, is correlated with a character which spans the range from the primitive to the civilised, and in falling partially under Iago's spell Othello yields to those elements in man that oppose civilised order (p. 139).

Despite his recognition of 'those elements in man that oppose civilised order', Evans fails to stress that the destructive impulses in the play emanate primarily from Iago and later in the article he appears to confuse traditional literary colour denotations with overt racial categorisation. He describes Desdemona and Othello in this way:

Desdemona dies . . . because of a naiveté that exceeds her own . . . *Considering the factors of age, race, and above all, the lover's simplicity, ordinary realism suggests this marriage was doomed from the start* . . . for much of Othello's second phase, a picture of the violent, jealous, credulous, 'uncivilised' Moor reverting to type dominates the play . . . [however] the *darkness* in the bedroom is not complete but is broken by an enduring vision of Desdemona's *whiteness* (pp. 135–6, p. 138; my emphasis).

As I suggested earlier, such interpretations of *Othello* result partly from the tendency to treat Othello as a character in isolation from the context in which Shakespeare sets him in the play, and in isolation from the problems identified by the language of all those who speak besides, as well as includ-

109

ing, the general. Whenever this is done, something has to be found to explain the character and actions of the hero. Although Shakespeare himself sees the tragedy as primarily lying elsewhere than in Othello (as a 'black' man), such analyses, ignoring this in their attempt to arraign the hero, recently appear to have become more and more desperate. One fairly new article, which quotes with apparent approbation both Lerner and Leavis, not only finds Othello to be strongly sensual, vindictively jealous and ferociously stupid, but contorts the character at the same time into someone both sexually frustrated and sexually unsuccessful![89]

8

None of these critics, it may be claimed, was necessarily desirous of being racist when he wrote. But the danger is that we leave unidentified, except perhaps in passing, these under-currents and their implications in such work — as if to register them would be an exercise in bad taste. Whatever the case may be elsewhere, in South Africa silence about so tenacious a tendency in *Othello* criticism has the effect of a not-too-covert expression of support for prevailing racist doctrines.

For those in South Africa who abhor the dominant *apartheid* ideology and its practice, *Othello* has special importance. Indeed, Othello's reference to his being 'sold to slavery' and to his 'redemption thence' (I. iii. 138), during his account of his early life, cannot be taken by a South African audience as a purely incidental remark.[90] Like the extensive concern with colour in the play and the colonial context from Act II on, the brief mention of slavery directs us to that faculty in man for destruction and exploitation. And in South Africa slavery was one of the crucial factors contributing to the growth of racist ideology. The South African historians Du Toit and Giliomee describe the impact of slavery upon Cape society in this way:

As the number of slaves increased in the eighteenth century, the effects of slavery began to permeate the entire social order. The belief became

110

entrenched that the proper role of the white inhabitants was to be a land- and slave-owning élite, and that manual or even skilled labour in the service of someone else did not befit anyone with the status of freeman. Slavery, then, came to inform the meaning of other status groups as well. Cardozo remarked that in a slave society freedom is defined by slavery; thus everyone aspired to have slaves. With respect to the Cape an observer remarked in 1743: 'Having imported slaves, every common or ordinary European becomes a gentleman and prefers to be served than to serve . . . The majority of farmers in the Cape are not farmers in the real sense of the word . . . and many of them consider it a shame to work with their hands.'[91]

The quotation from a nineteenth-century South African response to *Othello*, with which I began this chapter, was actually published when the Great Trek, which was at least in part a response to the abolition of slavery, had just begun. Some of the Trekker leaders resisted the abolition precisely because it removed forms of social discrimination. Karel Trichardt, for instance, noting his people's reactions to the abolition, emphasises that 'the main objection to the new dispensation was the equalisation of coloured people with the whites,' and Anna Steenkamp, the niece of another Voortrekker leader, protested that the emancipation of slaves involved:

their equalization with the Christians, in conflict with the laws of God and the natural divisions of descent and faith, so that it became unbearable for any decent Christian to submit to such a burden; we therefore preferred to move in order to be able the better to uphold our faith and the Gospel in an unadulterated form.[92]

Such distasteful attitudes are likely to have resulted from the loss of that position of exploitation which Du Toit and Giliomee identify. Indeed the theorist Harold Wolpe has stressed the importance of the connection between racism and the context in which it occurs:

The failure to examine the changing non-ideological conditions in which specific groups apply and therefore interpret and therefore modify their ideologies results in treating the latter as unchanging . . . entities. By simply ascribing all action to generalised racial beliefs,

111

prejudices or ideologies, the specific content of changing social relations and the conditions of change become excluded from analysis.[93]

It is interesting to note, in the context of the Trekkers' reaction to the abolition of slavery, Ashley Montagu's description of those opponents of emancipation beyond South Africa who began to exploit racism as a tactic against reform: 'The idea of "race" was in fact the deliberate creation of an exploiting class which was seeking to maintain and defend its privileges against what was profitably regarded as an inferior social caste.'[94] He cites the example that 'as an investment the "inferior caste" yielded a profit which on the average amounted to thirty per cent' (p. 39).

Many factors may have contributed to the growth of racism in South Africa, but the use of racist mythology to justify or mask exploitation seems to be one of the society's most consistent features. To take only one further instance: the exploitative classes who came to South Africa in the last years of the nineteenth and early twentieth century found racism convenient in a context from which they, too, were materially to benefit enormously. In an address to the South African Colonisation Society, one Sir Matthew Nathan, for instance, had this to say on the subject of black nurses: 'Just as natives had a peculiar exterior so they had a peculiar character, and it was obvious that the British colonist did not want his child imbued with the ideas of a lower civilisation.'[95]

Other recorded observations, then and since, from those who stood most to profit from the 'implications' of racism, communicate attitudes almost identical, often, to those Shakespeare gives to Iago.[96] To a degree, too, Iago's mode of operation anticipates what later social historians and theorists identify as racist behaviour. Iago's and Roderigo's colour prejudice is recognised as sordid, the resort of men who in one way or another feel mediocre and overlooked. Iago uses racism against an individual whose skills, ability and success in crucial ways exceed his own. And he uses it as a tactic — when he believes it may afford him some material advantage over the man whom he wishes to control and if possible destroy.

9

Both Hunter and Jones have provided evidence to suggest that in the treatment of colour there were also non-racist currents in iconography and literature and it is to such currents that *Othello* may be said to contribute. Thus Hunter shows that the convention of portraying one of the three Magi in iconography as black emerges as early as the eighth century.[97] Hunter notes too that the sense that 'black-faced foreigners might in fact be figures from a more innocent world close to Christianity grew apace in the Renaissance' (p. 155). A Portuguese painting of the Epiphany, which he mentions in his discussion, depicts a Brazilian chief in full regalia instead of the black Balthazar.[98] As Eldred Jones indicates, travel writing too was not always based upon racist fictions, but sometimes mixed with scientific observation.[99] Writing about the New World, especially, was most eloquently dismissive of judgements based upon colour prejudice. For instance, the appalling treatment of the natives of the Americas — seen as innocents — by their so-called civilised colonisers prompted Fulke Greville to observe:

in stead of spreading Christian religion by good life, [the Spaniards] committed such terrible inhumanities as gave those that lived under nature manifest occasion to abhor the devilry character of so tyrannical a deity [as the Christian God].[100]

Perhaps it is worth resting in this matter of *Othello* and racism upon two further extracts, each of which confirms that Shakespeare's play was, in the attitudes it suggests, not an isolated argument against the racist tendencies of his world. The first comes predictably from Montaigne's famous essay, 'Of the Caniballes', based on his own experience of the natives of America, which prompted him, on the subject of human dignity to observe that 'there is nothing in that nation, that is either barbarous or savage, unless men call that barbarisme which is not common to them'.[101] The influence of Montaigne in *The Tempest* is often identified but it is not as often recalled that, apart from the similarity in attitudes to be found in Montaigne's essay and *Othello*, Florio had translated the essays into English in 1603, the year before Shakespeare is likely to have written his play. Whether or not Shakespeare had by then read the original, the appearance of the translation must have been an event to emphasise, at least, Montaigne's importance. One of the many passages that by implication strongly attacks racist modes of thought reads:

I am sorie *Lycurgus* and *Plato* had [no knowledge of the societies of the New World] for me seemeth that what in those nations we see by experience, doth not only exceed all the pictures wherewith licentious Poesie hath proudly imbellished the golden age, and all her quaint inventions to faine a happy condition of man, but also the conception and desire of Philosophy. They could not imagine a genuitie so pure and simple, as we see it by experience; nor ever beleeve our societie might be maintained with so little art and humane combination. It is a nation, would I answer *Plato*, that hath no kind of traffike, no knowledge of Letters, no intelligence of numbers, no name of magistrate, nor of politike superioritie; no use of service, of riches or of povertie; no contracts, no successions, no partitions, no occupation but idle; no respect of kinred, but common, no apparell but naturall, no manuring of lands, no use of wine, corne, or mettle. The very words that import lying, falshood, treason, dissimulations, covetousnes, envie, detraction, and pardon, were never heard of amongst them. How dissonant would hee finde his imaginarie commonwealth from this perfection! (p. 164)

Again, in the second passage, another writer responds to the multiplicity of skin pigmentation he has encountered in his travels, without prejudice but with a sense of wonder at what he interprets to be evidence of his God's bounty:

One of the marvellous things that God useth in the composition of man is colour, which doubtless can not be considered without great admiration in beholding one to be white, and another black, being colours utterly contrary. Some likewise to be yellow . . . as men are commonly white in Europe and black in Africa, even with like variety are they tawny in these Indies, with divers degrees diversely inclining more or less to black or white . . . It may seem that such variety of colours proceedeth of man, and not of the earth, which may well be although we be all born of Adam and Eve, and know not the cause why God hath ordained it, otherwise than to consider that his divine majesty hath done this as infinite other to declare his omnipotence and wisdom in such diversity of colours as appear not only in the nature of man, but the like also in beasts, birds and flowers, where diverse and contrary colours are seen in one little feather, or the leaves growing out of one little stalk.[102]

10

Certain of the English and American readings of *Othello* I have noted should stand as a warning as to the ease with which racism may obscure the play's concerns. Thus for some critics within an English audience that has seen not only the institution and abolition of slavery but the rise and decline of a colonial empire, there have sometimes been problems. What then must happen to a South African audience for so long under the hegemony of a dominant class that has entrenched racism in its ideology?

The danger is not merely that the colonial context insisted on by the dramatic situation from Act II on will be ignored. That context identifies the ruling agent of the dominant order as someone who looks as if he comes from the 'other', either the subordinate orders or the alien cultures that lie beyond and which may threaten the periphery of state power. Yet the text is careful to demonstrate that this agent of the dominant order, in terms both of loyalty and inner beliefs, belongs to the ruling class. Nevertheless, the text shows that away from the ruler, and on the periphery of state power, violent antagonisms and impulses to disruption exist within, not beyond, the military/colonial apparatus. Moreover, the primary thrust to dominance, by means partly of disruption and violence, within this apparatus, comes from one of the servants of that commander whose own service to the state is presented as exemplary. Alarmingly, that subordinate agent is effective. The means he uses, the application of narrative in an improvisatory and exploitative way, the manipulation of judicial procedures, the use of doctrines of loyalty and honesty to legitimate (and conceal) his behaviour — and all of these in order to dominate and subordinate, to

115

attain mastery — prompts inferences about the behaviour of the dominant order itself, certainly about the colonial and military apparatus, *in situ*, on the periphery, not only in terms of what operates within it, but in its actual dealings both with subordinate orders and alien cultures.

The danger for South African audiences, however, is also that even within more traditional approaches to the text, crucial issues will be hedged. Thus the confusion and passion, the turbulence that results from the central human dilemma which the text may be said, in terms of traditional Christian discourse about a fallen world, to activate by means of the intervention of Iago is not addressed. Instead Othello's 'over passionate', 'over violent' *nature*, his 'jealousy' and 'egocentricity', his 'bombast' and his 'stupidity' — all the racist accusations brought to bear against the man personally appear; the text's concern, in a fallen world, with the human subject's limited faculties for perception as well as judgement, concomitant problems of appearance and reality, and the consequent inevitable vulnerability of individuals to error and to exploitation on a private, social and judicial level, vanishes.

In South Africa, the so-called Immorality Act, which forbade relationships between peoples of different colour and which was only recently, in 1985, apparently abandoned, was peripheral in its impact upon the majority of South Africans, as compared with the many other more crucially destructive laws which have served the interests of the dominant order. Yet because of the attempt it made to legislate upon, interfere with and exploit for purposes of control, human desire and love it retains a symbolic repugnance. *Othello* must still be experienced within the shadow of this Act and, more important, the larger system of which it formed part. Athol Fugard's *Statements After an Arrest Under the Immorality Act* is one of the many attempts occurring in the literature of this country to portray the way in which the dominant order may utilise racism and the law in order to demonise human sexuality and in so doing reinforce its own authority. *Othello* too presents the destruction of a love relationship in which, in very different ways specific to its own context, racism and the abuse of the legal process plays a terrible part. Nevertheless, in its fine scrutiny of the mechanisms underlying Iago's use of colour prejudice, and in its rejection of human pigmentation as a means of identifying worth, the play, as it always has done, continues to oppose racism.

Notes

1 S. Plaatje, 'A South African's Homage' in I. Gollancz, *A Book of Homage to Shakespeare* (Oxford: Oxford University Press, 1916), pp. 336–9 cited in *English in Africa*, 3:2, 1976, p. 8. Stephen Gray, 'Plaatje's Shakespeare', *English in Africa*, 4:1, 1977, p. 4, gives an account of Plaatje's translations. Plaatje is the author of *Native Life in South Africa* (London: P.S. King and Son Ltd., 1916).

2 Quoted in Eric Rosenthal, 'Early Shakespearean Productions in South Africa', *English Studies in Africa,* 7:2, 1974, p. 210.

3 Eric Rosenthal, 'Early Shakespearean Productions in South Africa', p. 210.

4 Eldred Jones, *Othello's Countrymen* (London: Oxford University Press, 1965), pp. 12–13.

5 Winthrop D. Jordan, *The White Man's Burden: Historical Origins of Racism in the United States* (New York: Oxford University Press, 1974), pp. 3–4. Jordan notes (p. 35) 'from about 1550 Englishmen were in such continual contact with the Spanish that they could hardly have failed to acquire the notion that Negroes could be enslaved.'

6 V. G. Kiernan, 'European attitudes to the outside world' in *'Race' in Britain — Continuity and Change,* ed. Charles Husband (London: Hutchinson, 1982), pp. 27, 29. The proverb is mentioned by G.K. Hunter, *'Othello* and Colour Prejudice', *Proceedings of the British Academy,* 53, 1967 (London: Oxford University Press, 1968), pp. 139–63.

7 Jordan, *The White Man's Burden,* p. 22.

8 G.K. Hunter's essay *'Othello* and Colour Prejudice' is excellent as is Eldred Jones's highly informative work *Othello's Countrymen.* See also Jones, *The Elizabethan Image of Africa* Charlottesville: University of Virginia Press, 1971).

9 Doris Adler, 'The Rhetoric of *Black* and *White* in *Othello',* *Shakespeare Quarterly,* 25, 1974, pp. 248–57, has offered a highly sensitive account of the multiple resonances in the use of the words

'black', 'white', and 'fair'. Whilst I agree with almost everything in this valuable article, I intend to argue that although Othello does appear partly to 'describe himself in terms of (Iago's) racial stereotype' (p. 254), his primary dilemma in the play relates to Iago's refashioning of Desdemona's image. See also Harold Clarke Goddard, 'Othello and the Race Problem' in Alphabet of the Imagination (Atlantic Highlands, N.J.: Humanities Press, 1974), pp. 74–84.

10 Hunter, 'Othello and Colour Prejudice', p. 145. Hunter notes that 'there were Moors in London Lord Mayor's Pageants in 1519, 1521, 1536, 1541, 1551, 1589, 1609, 1611, 1624.'

11 Jones, Othello's Countrymen, pp. 31–3.

12 Jones, Othello's Countrymen, pp. 40–68.

13 An account of John Lok's voyages first published by Eden in 1554–55 and reprinted 1577 and 1589. The note forms part of Eden's own added account and is cited in Jones, Othello's Countrymen, p. 11.

14 Jones, Othello's Countrymen, pp. 14, 40–9.

15 Cited in Jones, Othello's Countrymen, p. 8.

16 Cited in Jones, Othello's Countrymen, p. 22.

17 It might be argued that the term 'colour prejudice' is more appropriate for the sixteenth and seventeenth centuries than the term 'racism'. It may, however, be argued equally that from the perspective of the twentieth century the term 'colour prejudice' is not profitably to be distinguished from the modern sense of racist practice. The one implies, if it does not always lead to, the other. As early as the sixteenth century, active exploitation/persecution on the basis of colour was, in any event, under way. Oliver Cromwell Cox, 'Race and Exploitation: A Marxist View' in Race and Social Difference, ed. Paul Baxter and Basil Sansom (Harmondsworth: Penguin, 1972), pp. 205–20, describes Sepulveda, who, in 1550 attempted to justify the right of the Spaniards to wage wars against the Indians as 'among the first great racists; his argument was, in effect, that the Indians were inferior to the Spaniards, therefore they should be exploited' (p. 210). In this chapter, the terms 'colour prejudice' and 'racism' and their variants are used interchangeably.

18 All references to Othello are from The Riverside Shakespeare, gen. ed. G. Blakemore Evans (Boston: Houghton Mifflin, 1974). References are to act, scene and line. Where more than one line is quoted, the number for the 'last' quoted line is given.

19 Stone, The Crisis of the Aristocracy, pp. 591–2.

20 Keith Wrightson, *English Society 1580—1660* (London: Hutchinson, 1982), p. 73.

21 The Duke's comment at I. iii. 289—90 is discussed below.

22 This is not to claim an infallible Desdemona. Jane Adamson, *Othello as tragedy: some problems of judgement and feeling* (Cambridge: Cambridge University Press, 1980), pp. 214—63.
identifies the extent to which Desdemona's own misunderstanding of her husband and her misjudgement of the situation help to compound the errors in which all become embroiled. One of the best articles on the quality of the relationship between Desdemona and Othello, and lucid and helpful in many other ways too, is G.M. Matthews's, '*Othello* and the Dignity of Man' in *Shakespeare in a Changing World*, ed. Arnold Kettle, pp. 122—45: 'Both lovers assert "humane" values against the conventions that debase them' (p. 129).

23 Jordan, *The White Man's Burden,* p. 20.

24 Adamson, *Othello as tragedy,* p. 96.

25 William Elton, *King Lear and the Gods* (California: The Huntington Library, 1966), p. 137.

26 Giraldi's Moor 'lacks most of the dimensions of the tragic hero' (Kenneth Muir, *Shakespeare's Sources,* London: Methuen, 1965, vol. 1, p. 126) but the story provided Shakespeare, once he had made the necessary changes, with the opportunity to explore his concern with the limits of human judgement and the consequent problem of perspicacity.

27 T. Sipahigil, 'Lewkenor and Othello: an Addendum', *Notes and Queries,* 19:4, 1972, p. 127, draws attention to Malone's stress, in Sir Lewis Lewkenor's translation *The Commonwealth and Government of Venice* (1599), upon the words 'alwaies they do entertain in honourable sort with great provision a *captain generall,* who alwaies is *a stranger borne'.* Sipahigil quotes certain other passages which emphasise the prestige and power of the captain general, and highlights Shakespeare's adaptation of what in Cinthio is a 'routine change of troops maintained by Venice in Cyprus involving a captain and his soldiers leaving in a single ship' into 'the urgent commissioning of a general who departs with an undisclosed number of ships for an imminent naval engagement'.

28 *Antony and Cleopatra,* ed. M.R. Ridley (London: Methuen, 1982) p. 29.

29 Stephen Greenblatt, *Renaissance Self-Fashioning* (Chicago: The University of Chicago Press, 1980), pp. 246—7.

30 Simonds D'Ewes, quoted in Stone, *The Crisis of the Aristocracy,*

p. 665.

31 Jones, *Othello's Countrymen,* pp. 49—60, 68—71.

32 All references to *The Merchant of Venice* are taken from *The Merchant of Venice,* ed. John Russell Brown (London: Methuen, 1979).

33 R.C. Bald, 'The Booke of Sir Thomas More and its Problems', *Shakespeare Survey* 2, 1949, pp. 44—65; pp. 52—3, observes that 'almost every possible date between 1586 and 1605 has at one time or other been suggested . . . the more extreme limits can doubtless be ignored. Disturbances against foreigners, though not on the scale of the insurrection which More is alleged to have pacified, are recorded for the years 1586, 1593 and 1595—96, but one would expect the play to have been written at a discreet interval after, rather than on the heels of, such an outbreak . . . the general tendency has been to date *Sir Thomas More* c.1595—96 . . .' but G.B. Harrison's 'general contention for a date c.1600 rather than c.1595 on metrical grounds is well founded'.

34 *Shakespeare's Hand in the Play of 'Sir Thomas More'* (Cambridge: Cambridge University Press, 1923). Papers by Alfred W. Pollard, W.W. Greg, E. Maude Thompson, J. Dover Wilson and R.W. Chambers, p. 162.

35 *Papers,* A.W. Pollard *et al,* pp. 211—13.

36 Hunter, *'Othello* and Colour Prejudice', p. 153.

37 This is not the place to trace the careful process of suggestion, argument, retreat and qualification by which Iago proceeds — as an 'honest' witness, as a masterly and skilful abuser of rhetoric, and as the ensign who must with his superior tread very warily indeed. However, I agree with those critics who have shown the superficiality and carelessness in readings of this scene such as that offered by F.R. Leavis (to be referred to again later in this chapter). John Holloway, *The Story of the Night* (London: Routledge and Kegan Paul, 1961), pp. 155—65, offers what is still one of the most convincing refutations of the Leavis claim that Othello's response to Iago's suggestions in this scene is prompt and totally gullible.

38 I refer to both these critics again later in this chapter.

39 Paul A. Jorgensen, *Redeeming Shakespeare's Words* (California: University of California Press, 1962), pp. 3—21.

40 Jorgensen, *Redeeming Shakespeare's Words,* pp. 6—7, p. 10, describes *A Knack to Know a Knave* as featuring 'the character Honesty, a personified abstraction, who . . . is gifted with a knack for detecting knaves and offers his professional services to [the king] . . . Honesty is successful in exposing and flagellating several

knaves of the kind, typically presented as being injurious to a kingdom.'

41 'The "office" here might easily be mistaken by modern readers for Iago's military rank; almost certainly Iago meant his function as Honesty' (Jorgensen, *Redeeming Shakespeare's Words*, p. 18).

42 *Macbeth,* ed. K. Muir (London: Methuen, 1970).

43 *The Works of Robert Boyle* (1690), V (London: 1772), 529, cited in Barbara J. Shapiro, *Probability and Certainty in Seventeenth Century England* (Princeton: Princeton University Press, 1983), p. 179.

44 Shapiro, *Probability and Certainty in Seventeenth Century England,* p. 194, p. 198.

45 *The Triall of Witchcraft* (1616), pp. 80—1, cited in Shapiro, p. 201. On legislation against witchcraft see C. L'Estrange Ewen ed., *Witch Hunting and Witch Trials. The Indictments for Witchcraft from the Records of 1373 Assizes held for the Home Circuit AD 1559—1736.* (London: Kegan Paul, Trench, Trubner and Co., 1929), pp. 13, 15, 19.

46 According to Greenblatt, 'improvisation' is 'the ability both to capitalise on the unforeseen and to transform given materials into one's own scenario' (pp. 224—8). I refer again to this definition later in the chapter. Ruth Cowhig, 'The Importance of Othello's Race', *Journal of Commonwealth Literature*, 2, 1977, pp. 153—61, argues that the audience witnesses in part 'the baiting of an alien who cannot fight back on equal terms' (p. 157).

47 Adamson, *Othello as tragedy,* p. 19.

48 'Justice and Love in *Othello*', *University of Toronto Quarterly, 21,* 1952, p. 339. Ruth Cowhig, 'The Importance of Othello's Race', observes: '*Othello* was very closely followed by *King Lear,* and in both plays Shakespeare seems to be exploring the basic nature of man, and especially the effect on that nature of the subservience of reason to the passions' (p. 159).

49 The *natural* vulnerability of goodness to hidden malice is under-lined as a central concern in the play in the account of Desde-mona's escape from the storm, when Cassio speaks of 'The gutter'd rocks and congregated sands,/Traitors ensteep'd to enclog the guilt-less keel' (II. i. 70).

50 Muir, *Shakespeare's Sources,* pp. 122—40.

51 Frederic C. Lane, *Venice: A Maritime Republic* (Baltimore: Johns Hopkins University Press, 1973), pp. 297—8. I rely in this chapter upon certain arguments in the work of Immanuel Wallerstein. Wallerstein, *The Capitalist World-Economy* (Cambridge: Cambridge

University Press, 1979), writes about the nascent European world economy of the sixteenth century: 'The way the European world-economy operated in bare outline was simple enough. The geographical limits of this world-economy, determined largely by the state of technology at the time, included northwest Europe, which became the core of the system during this period, eastern Europe (but not Russia) which, along with Spanish America, became its periphery, and the Christian Mediterranean area which, having been at the outset an advanced core area, became transformed in the course of the sixteenth century into a semiperiphery' (p. 38). Wallerstein defines his terms as follows: 'Core, semiperiphery and periphery all refer to positions in the economic system. The core areas were the location of a complex variety of economic activities — mass-market industries such as there were (mainly textiles and shipbuilding), international and local commerce in the hands of an *indigenous* bourgeoisie, relatively advanced and complex forms of agriculture ... The peripheral areas, by contrast, were monocultural, with the cash crops being produced on large estates by coerced labour. The semiperipheral areas were in the process of deindustrializing. The form of agricultural labour control they used was intermediate between the freedom of the lease system and the coercion of slavery and serfdom. It was for the most part share-cropping ... The semiperiphery, in transition, still retained for the time being some share in international banking and high-cost quality industrial production' (p. 38).

52 Lane, *Venice*, p. 298.

53 Louis B. Wright, 'Colonial Developments in the Reign of James I' in *The Reign of James VI and I*, ed. A.G.R. Smith (London: Macmillan, 1973), pp. 123—39, mentions Sir Humphrey Gilbert and his half-brother Sir Walter Raleigh: 'Gilbert, by claiming Newfoundland for England in 1583, helped to fix interest upon that region. Raleigh, by his experiences and his establishment of the short-lived colonies on the coast of North Carolina in 1585—87, kept alive interest in "Virgina" ... The English were also fascinated by possibilities of colonisation in the tropics. Raleigh personally led an expedition up the Orinoco River as far as the falls of the Rio Caroni in 1595 ... Raleigh's descriptive narrative, *The Discovery of the Large, Rich and Beautiful Empire of Guiana* (1596), expressed his own enthusiasm for the country and influenced Englishmen in the reign of James I to attempt to colonise in tropical America' (p. 123). Jordan, *The White Man's Burden*, writes 'Richard Hakluyt ... roused enthusiasm for western planting and ...

stirred the nation with his monumental compilation *The Principal Navigations, Voyages, Traffiques and Discoveries of the English Nation . . . '* (p. 3).

54 Wright, 'Colonial Developments in the Reign of James I', p. 124. The Muscovy Company was created in 1555; Antony Jenkinson's journey was undertaken in 1557–59 (p. 124). Robert Ashton, *The City and the Court 1603–1643* (Cambridge: Cambridge University Press, 1979) cites, among many others, the example of Sir Thomas Smythe: 'Governor for fifteen years in all of the East India Company, he was also in his time governor of the Russia, French, Levant, Virginia and Somers Islands companies' (pp. 16–17).

55 Wright, 'Colonial Developments in the Reign of James I', p. 124. The East India Company received its charter on 31 December 1600; the net return to investors from this first expedition was '95 per cent' (p. 124). 'A second expedition led by Sir Henry Middleton returned in 1606 and proved almost as profitable' (p. 124). Discussing the expansion of Europe in the sixteenth century, Immanuel Wallerstein, *The Modern World-System: Capitalist Agriculture and the Origins of the European World-Economy in the Sixteenth Century* (New York: Academic Press, 1974), notes the pressure on Europe to expand at this time, and 'to expand successfully is a function both of the ability to maintain relative social solidarity at home (in turn a function of the mechanisms of the distribution of reward) and the arrangements that can be made to use *cheap* labour *far away* (it being all the more important that it be cheap the further it is away, because of transport costs)' (pp. 85–6). It is worth noting some of Wallerstein's other categories here: 'The world economy at this time had various kinds of workers: There were slaves who worked on sugar plantations and in easy kinds of mining operations . . . There were 'serfs' who worked on large domains where grain was cultivated and wood harvested. There were 'tenant' farmers on various kinds of cash-crop operations (including grain) and wage labourers, in some agricultural production . . . In addition there was a small layer of intermediate personnel — supervisors of labourers, independent artisans, a few skilled workmen — and a thin layer of ruling classes, occupied in overseeing large land operations, operating major institutions of the social order, and to some extent pursuing their own leisure. This last group included both the existing nobility and the patrician bourgeoisie (as well as, of course, the Christian clergy and the state bureaucracy)' (p. 86). The world economy was based on the assumption that there were different modes of labour suitable to

different zones of the world economy 'to assure the kind of flow of the surplus which enabled the capitalist system to come into existence' (p. 87). Part of the reason for the movement of sugar cultivation to the Atlantic islands and then to Brazil and the West Indies was the exhaustion of labour supplies. Nevertheless the rudimentary elements of the system must have operated at the time Venice was ascendant. Wallerstein, for instance, describes the 'feudalisms' of sixteenth-century Eastern Europe and Hispanic America in this way: 'the landowner (seignior) was producing for a capitalist world-economy. The economic limits of his exploitative pressure were determined by the demand-supply curve of a market. He was maintained in power by the strength rather than the weakness of the central authority, at least its strength *vis à vis* the farm labourer' (p. 91). The peasants in this system 'are required by some legal process enforced by the state to labor at least part of the time on a large domain producing some product for sale on the world market. Normally the domain was the "possession" of an individual, usually by designation of the state, but not necessarily a heritable property . . . this form of labour control became the dominant one in agricultural production in the peripheral areas of the sixteenth-century European world-economy' (p. 91). 'The pattern already began with the Venetians in Crete and elsewhere in the fourteenth century and became widespread by the sixteenth century throughout the periphery and semi-periphery of the European world-economy' (p. 92).

56 Brian Dietz, 'England's Overseas Trade in the Reign of James I' in *The Reign of James VI and I,* ed. A.G.R. Smith, pp. 106—22, p. 115.

57 James began negotiations with Spain on his accession in 1603, which led to peace in 1604.

58 Wright, 'Colonial Developments in the Reign of James I', writes that Raleigh's early 'emphasis on silk, cotton, dye-stuff, pepper, sugar, ginger and other commodities would find constant iteration in later advocates of colonisation. These and other exotic products England had to buy from economic competitors — sometimes her enemies — at a great loss to the nation. Colonies might prove to be the remedy. The hope of discovering vast hoards of gold and silver, as the Spaniards had done, was never completely abandoned by Elizabethan and Jacobean adventurers overseas, but gradually they came to realise that profits from trade were more certain, and the production of exotic products within a colonial framework might confer great national benefits' (p. 125).

59 Ashton, *The City and the Court 1603—1643,* pp. 34—5, shows that of the twenty-eight aldermen of London serving at one time or another in 1603 at least half had come to have directive interests in overseas investment, twenty-two had interests in overseas trade, eighteen had interests in more than one branch of overseas trade.

60 Wallerstein, *The Capitalist World-Economy,* p. 42.

61 Wallerstein, *The Capitalist World-Economy,* pp. 45—8.

62 Paul Brown, ' "This thing of darkness I acknowledge mine": *The Tempest* and the discourse of colonialism' in *Political Shakespeare* ed. Jonathan Dollimore and Alan Sinfield (Manchester: Manchester University Press, 1985), pp. 48—71, provides useful references and information on the subject.

63 For an account of this see Jones, *Othello's Countrymen,* pp. 1—26.

64 See Jordan, *The White Man's Burden,* pp. 22—5.

65 Brown, ' "This thing of darkness I acknowledge mine": *The Tempest* and the discourse of colonialism', pp. 50—1.

66 See note 51 and note 55.

67 Brown, ' "This thing of darkness I acknowledge mine": *The Tempest* and the discourse of colonialism', p. 52.

68 Brown, ' "This thing of darkness I acknowledge mine": *The Tempest* and the discourse of colonialism', writes: 'colonialist discourse voices a demand both for order and disorder, producing a disruptive other in order to assert the superiority of the coloniser. Yet that production is itself evidence of a struggle to restrict the other's disruptiveness to that role. Colonialist discourse does not simply announce a triumph for civility, it must continually *produce* it, and this work involves struggle and risk' (p. 58).

69 Greenblatt, *Renaissance Self-Fashioning,* pp. 222—54.

70 Greenblatt, *Renaissance Self-Fashioning,* p. 234 ff.

71 Greenblatt, *Renaissance Self-Fashioning,* p. 242 ff.

72 Some of the implications of such a removal of the ruler are explored in chapter 4.

73 Stephen Greenblatt, *Renaissance Self-Fashioning,* pp. 185—6.

74 Geoffrey Hutchings, 'Emilia: A Case History in Women's Lib', *English Studies in Africa,* 21, 1978, pp. 71—7.

75 C.O. Gardner, 'Tragic Fission in *Othello'*, pp. 11—25.

76 Husband ed., *'Race' in Britain — Continuity and Change,* p. 19.

77 Helen Gardner, 'The Noble Moor', *Proceedings of The British Academy,* 41, 1955 (London: Oxford University Press, 1955).

78 T.S. Eliot, 'Shakespeare and the Stoicism of Seneca' in *Selected Essays,* 3rd ed. (London: Faber and Faber, 1958), p. 130.

79 F.R. Leavis, 'Diabolic Intellect and the Noble Hero' in *The Common Pursuit* (Harmondsworth: Peregrine, 1962), pp. 136—59.

80 The programme note to the National Theatre production of *Othello* (London: The National Theatre, 1964), with Sir Laurence Olivier as Othello and Frank Finlay as Iago, production by John Dexter, performed at the Old Vic during the 1964—65 season, quotes extensively from Leavis's essay and includes most of the passages to which I refer in my discussion, together with many others, germane to the present point, which I do not quote.

81 Thomas Rymer, 'A Short View of Tragedy' (1693), extracts reprinted in *Shakespeare, The Critical Heritage,* ed. Brian Vickers, 2 (London: Routledge and Kegan Paul, 1974), p. 51.

82 Terence Hawkes ed., *Coleridge on Shakespeare* (Harmondsworth: Penguin, 1969), p. 188.

83 The beginnings of the great debate about Othello's colour go back to the late eighteenth century. In a letter to *The Gentleman's Magazine,* 61, 1791, Verbum Sat (pseud.) writes:

He is a *Moor,* and yet is always figured as a *Negro.* I need not tell that the *Moors,* or people of the North of Africa, are dusky, but with very agreeable features, and manly persons, and vigorous and ingenious minds; while the Negros [*sic*] have features remarkably unpleasant, mean persons, and little power of mind. I suspect that this ludicrous mistake proceeded from Shakespeare's speaking of the *blackness* of Othello's *complexion,* and indeed *face,* compared with the European: and I am convinced that is not older than the revival of the theatres in 1660 (pp. 225—6).

In 'Some Notes on Othello', *Cornhill Magazine,* 18, 1868, pp. 419—40, J.J. Elmes is one of the nineteenth-century writers who disagrees with Coleridge. Even so, he quotes Schlegel at one point:

We recognise in Othello the wild nature of that glowing zone which generates the most ravenous beasts of prey and the most deadly poisons, tamed only in appearance by the desire of fame, by foreign laws of honour, and by nobler and milder manners (p. 438).

and he underlines later the 'repugnance, more generally felt than expressed, to a negro being the hero of a love story' (p. 438). See also Francis Jacox's opening remarks in *Shakespeare Diversions, Second Series: From Dogberry to Hamlet* (1877), pp. 73—5 and Cumberland Clark, *Shakespeare and National Character: A study of Shakespeare's knowledge and dramatic and literary use of the distinctive racial characteristics of the different peoples of the world* (London: Hamlin, 1932):

In spite of his intercourse with the polite world, which had produced that westernised veneer so easily assumed by the coloured races, Othello is still barbarian bred with instincts that suddenly break forth in ungovernable impulse (p. 229).

The debate about a tawny or black Othello lingers on as recently as Philip Butcher, 'Othello's Racial Identity', *Shakespeare Quarterly*, 3, 1952, pp. 243–7, who argues: 'Brabantio is not merely annoyed because his consent was not asked. Only a black Othello can serve as adequate motivation for his attitude towards his daughter's marriage to a man of exalted rank and reputation' (p. 244). Arthur Herman Wilson's letter to *Shakespeare Quarterly*, 4, 1953, p. 209 contests this. Ruth Cowhig, 'Actors, Black and Tawny, in the Role of Othello — and their Critics', *Theatre Research International* (Glasgow), 4, 1979, pp. 133–46, provides a historical survey of changing attitudes to the colour of Othello from the late eighteenth century on. I am most grateful to the late Professor John Hazel Smith for alerting me to the writers mentioned in this footnote.

84 A.C. Bradley, *Shakespearean Tragedy* (London: Macmillan, 1961), p. 165. Sanford E. Marovitz, 'Othello Unmasked: A Black Man's Conscience and a White Man's Fool', *Southern Review* (Adelaide), 6, 1973, pp. 108–37 identifies a similar tendency towards racist innuendo in the writing of Harley Granville Barker. The article itself, however, goes on to display ambiguity: the author identifies a conflict within Othello between a civilised self and a 'savage consciousness' (p. 124): 'The emotionalism and barbarity characteristic of the black stereotype at last wholly prevail over the cool, rational behaviour of the white Christian world which the alien Moor had adopted' (p. 125); 'Othello's rational soldier's mind, the mind of a white Christian, is overwhelmed' (p. 130); etc.

85 Arden edition, *Othello* (London: Methuen, 1958), p. li. See also pp. liii–liv.

86 Laurence Lerner, 'The Machiavel and the Moor', *Essays in Criticism*, 9, 1959, pp. 339–60.

87 See Tim Couzens, 'The Return of the Heart of Darkness', *The English Academy Review*, 1982, pp. 36–52.

88 K.W. Evans, 'The Racial Factor in *Othello*', *Shakespeare Studies*, 5, 1970, pp. 124–40.

89 T.G.A. Nelson and Charles Haines, 'Othello's Unconsummated Marriage', *Essays in Criticism*, 33, 1983, pp. 1–18. This is another attempt to pin on Othello a *personal* accusation to account for the tragedy. The authors base their claim that Othello is sexually frustrated and sexually unsuccessful on his never having consum-

mated his marriage with Desdemona. Disregarding the double time issue, given the fact that Shakespeare deliberately allows already established intimacy between Othello and Desdemona within the time span of the play itself to be interrupted, and given most significantly of all Iago's acknowledgement in pointedly inflammatory language at the beginning of the play that their marriage and its consummation has already taken place, their argument becomes at best highly disputable.

90 See note 5 above. In addition Samuel L. Macey, 'The Naming of the Protagonists in Shakespeare's *Othello*', *Notes and Queries*, 25:2, 1978, pp. 143—5, argues that Iago, a Spanish name, was a good choice because in northern eyes 'Spaniards were representatives of the devil' and because the name Iago was also suggestive of 'the patron saint of Spain who became widely known as the military man Santiago Matamoros, St James the Moor Killer'. It seems possible as well that the Spanish association may include an allusion to the Spanish role in America. The evidence in an article such as the one by Rodney Poisson, 'Othello's "Base Indian": A Better Source for the Allusion', *Shakespeare Quarterly*, 26, 1975, pp. 462—6, strengthens the argument that Shakespeare had the New World in mind when he wrote *Othello*.

91 Du Toit and Giliomee, *Afrikaner Political Thought: Analysis and Documents, 1780—1850* 1 (Cape Town: David Philip, 1983), p.7.

92 Cited in Heribert Adam and Hermann Giliomee, *The Rise and Crisis of Afrikaner Power* (Cape Town: David Philip, 1979), p. 95.

93 Cited in Dan O'Meara, *Volkskapitalisme* (Johannesburg: Ravan Press, 1983), p. 9.

94 A. Montagu, *Man's Most Dangerous Myth* (New York: Oxford University Press, 1974), p. 39.

95 Cited in Charles van Onselen, *Studies in the Social and Economic History of the Witwatersrand 1886—1914*, 2 (Johannesburg: Ravan Press, 1982), p. 29.

96 See 'Housewife', Van Onselen, p. 29. See also Charles O'Hara, cited in Van Onselen, p. 40.

97 Hunter, *'Othello* and Colour Prejudice', p. 154.

98 Hunter, *'Othello* and Colour Prejudice', writes: 'And so the old impulse to bring the Evangel to all nations acquired a new primitivist dynamic. An interesting demonstration of this is supplied in a Portuguese picture of the Epiphany c.1505 ... where a Brazilian chief, in full regalia, replaces the black Balthazar. Alongside the view that such black pagans could only acquire Christian hope by enslavement grew an alternative vision of their innocence as bring-

ing them near to God, by way of nature' (p. 155).

99 Jones, *Othello's Countrymen,* p. 8ff.
100 Cited in Hunter, '*Othello* and Colour Prejudice', p. 156.
101 Montaigne, 'Of the Caniballes' in *The Essayes of Montaigne* trans. John Florio, intro. J.I.M. Stewart (USA: The Modern Library, no date), p. 163.
102 From *The Decades of the New World or West India,* trans. Richard Eden (1555) in *The Literature of Renaissance England,* ed. John Hollander and Frank Kermode (New York: Oxford University Press, 1973), pp. 44—5.

4 Cruelty, *King Lear* and the South African Land Act 1913

Just before he has his eyes put out — in the scene which Dr Johnson described as 'too horrid to be endured in dramatick exhibition'[1] and which even as recent a critic as Harry Levin can describe as having only a 'certain propriety as a literal climax to a whole train of metaphors involving eyesight and suggesting moral perception'[2] — Gloucester, in reply to Regan's demand that he explain why he has sent King Lear to Dover, declares

> Because I would not see thy cruel nails
> Pluck out his poor old eyes; nor thy fierce sister
> In his anointed flesh rash boarish fangs.
>
> (III. vii. 57)[3]

At this moment Gloucester ceases completely to deal with the *de facto* power group within the ruling class. His direct statement of defiance aligns him with the hunted victims of that power — King Lear, without protection or shelter on the heath, and Edgar, proclaimed an outlaw throughout the land and disguised as Poor Tom.

The propriety of this scene to the concerns of *King Lear* is, however, more extensive than Levin's comment admits. He in fact also remarks that the scene presents a 'deliberate and definitive' breach of classical decorum — the Greeks preferred to have Oedipus's eyes put out off stage.[4] But he does not indicate that this 'breach of decorum' illustrates and embodies — in what we might call a terrifying, emblematic way — one aspect of the political thrust of the play. For in this scene the whole nexus of emerging relationships that *King Lear* explores, which, in the opening scene, involves a *shift* of power and which intensifies relentlessly in the scenes and acts to follow, comes to a point of awful clarity. Moreover, the interrogation and torture it presents set a seal on this process of change, identifying for the audience at the same time the essential nature of the *de facto* ruling power.

The phrase *de facto* is, however, inappropriate for the power which Goneril, Regan, and Edmund acquire in the first three acts. The text invests their possession of political power with elements of legality that cannot, really, be contested. For one thing, the daughters of Lear have each received, formally and legally, control of most of the kingdom; they have been granted this control by the King himself. Furthermore, the fugitive Edgar has been defined as an enemy of the ordered state, he is proclaimed as such and he is hunted by those functionaries concerned to uphold the current official notion of treachery. Even the 'court' that later tries Gloucester has claim to partial legality. The old duke has communicated treacherously with an invading army and he has in addition helped the King to join the foreign intruders.

Yet although we might note these facts, we recoil from the suggestion of legitimacy: *King Lear* stresses the extent to which the *shift* of power within the dominant order, initiated in Act I scene i, becomes at once also a *seizure* of power. It is sometimes forgotten that if Lear makes an appalling decision which proves to be mistaken, what follows is only possible because the conative dissembling of his two daughters enables them to acquire for themselves most of his domain. By the end of that first scene, furthermore, they indicate their determination to deprive him of the remaining material evidence of his authority. The first two acts — I. iii, I. iv, II. iv — depict this process moving ruthlessly to its conclusion. And this arrogation of power is complemented by scenes which alternate with those just noted. These portray Edmund's rapid ascendancy in a process which leads, by the end of Act III, to the displacement not only of his brother but of his father as well.

Why is there this ambiguity? Why does the text trouble to invest those who have in effect attached the apparatus of the state with what amounts to genuine legality?

1

In southern Africa one of the most influential and by now commonplace ways of interpreting this shift of power has been in terms of the conflict of ideas which Danby discusses in his work on the play published in 1948.[5] The conflict he identifies postulates on the one hand an 'orthodox' Elizabethan view, which sees 'nature' as

The same benign system [evident] in the temperate sunshine of Hooker's prose or in the dapplings of Bacon's allegory ... Nature like theirs is a structure ascending from primordial matter up to God. It, too, takes for granted that parents are to be honoured and human decencies observed. It assumes as the absolute shape for man an image of tenderness, comfort, generosity, charity, courtesy, gratitude (p. 28).

Such a view is on the other hand opposed, argues Danby, by notions influenced by writing such as Machiavelli's and writing anticipating Hobbes.[6] In this version, Man is outside of Nature:

Man, Nature, and God now fall apart. Reason, for Hooker the principle of coherence for all three, dwindles to something regulative rather than constitutive. It is an analyser, a cold calculator. Its knowledge is the knowledge of the watchmaker or engineer ... Nature itself becomes a machine this Reason can have this knowledge of ... Nature is inert and dead (pp. 44–5).

Consequently,

a thing's nature is laid down in its constitution — a stuff of matter and a propellant of appetite. We cannot change our nature or the nature of others. We can only express our nature, and others' natures we can use: for our own advantage ... every man is against every man (p. 45).

The application to the play by proponents of Danby of this view of a conflict of ideas suggests that traditional concepts involving notions of hierarchy and the Divine Right of Kings are to be seen as weakening under the onslaught of those who hold the newer ideas — usually portrayed negatively as in the case of Danby's use of epithets such as 'cold' and 'inert and dead'. The new approach defines political life purely as a struggle for power between partisan groups or individuals, and recommends in the efficient ruler, appropriate self-interest, the 'right' view of reason, and understanding of the weakness of man. Thus Danby comments:

Because the play is an allegory of ethical systems and people, it must also be an allegory of community. For according to one of the systems at least we are all members one of another. This society is that of the medieval vision. Its representative is an old King . . . It is doting and it falls into error. The other society is that of nascent capitalism. Its representative in chief is the New Man — and a politic machiavel (p. 52).

We need to recognise that although Danby registers the fact that *King Lear* is about change in Shakespeare's world, his language, with its emphasis upon the 'temperate' decencies and 'benign' divinely sanctioned order to be found in traditional notions tends to encourage the idealisation not only of these notions but of the system they are supposed to inform. His emphasis avoids the extent to which such traditional doctrines may provide the means, for the dominant order, of legitimating existing relations of domination and subordination. Moreover, as I have already remarked in previous chapters, historical debate has long since recognised that far from evidencing any fixed hierarchy, England in the sixteenth and seventeenth centuries was subject to a variety of conflicting pressures. The actual process of change in Shakespeare's age was complex; debate as to the exact nature of these changes and pressures, accompanied by great economic and social flux, has explored, among many other significant factors, the rise of the gentry, the decline of the aristocracy, or tensions between town gentry and country gentry.[7]

At one level, however, it may be argued that Danby's notion of conflict is to be found in the play. Edmund, Goneril and Regan are opposed in attitude and action to their counterparts within the dominant order whose language implies or alleges adherence to doctrines such as the Divine Right of Kings and hierarchy. And, from this point of view the text may be said to offer a dramatisation of what would happen if the groups holding the newer ideas, gaining material influence and seeking power, got out of hand. Moreover, in the context of such great fluidity involving the dissolution of old bonds and the creation of new relationships, the dominant class — so the Danbean influenced view might go — watching the play, would have been reassured by the construct represented by the now chivalrous Edgar, that appears to emerge at the conclusion. In terms of this, such a return to 'order' appears subdued but confident, apparently that if men but 'Speak what we feel, not what we ought to say' (V. iii. 324) the enormous complexities of the Jacobean social, political, and economic world would simplify themselves into the mythology of prescribed harmonies once more. This reading implies that the play evidences an act of consolidation. The returning Edgar signifies also a return to the traditional order, reflects the apparent work of providence and legitimates the position of the ruling class, with 'negative' elements expunged.

Such responses to the text in Europe and America have long since been modified or superseded, but in South Africa they continue. Although I have concentrated on Danby, the work of Tillyard has inevitably been important in influencing this process as well. The trend more particularly in South African versions of this critical response is to regard the plays as demonstrations of the surviving power of 'traditional' values. Thus in the article to which I referred briefly in chapter 1, 'Shakespeare Depoliticised', *King Lear* is said to reflect not merely medieval-influenced notions of the deforming power of sin, but to display in the presentation of Lear himself, recovery from sin. In another article written somewhat earlier, a different critic tends to avoid Act V almost completely. He concludes by emphasising Act IV scene vii to assert that in the context of the whole play:

Lear has gone through a complex of circumstances from which he can only emerge reformed and wise . . . The scene becomes suddenly a quiet kind of triumph for virtue . . . It is clearly, as happy an ending as one could want. The result . . . unifies . . . [it] reconciles the spiritual anxiety, sublimates the cruelty of the action by making its glaring pessimism a thing of beauty. This is Shakespeare's consistent mode in *King Lear* and the play's greatest source of power.[8]

As recently as 1985 a third South African critic, in an article concerned, tellingly, to demonstrate 'how the intense self-enclosed quality of Roman patriotism and stoicism led to certain life-denying impulses and attitudes' finds that such patriotism and stoicism seem at variance with 'the life-enhancing and richer social identity shown in the plays concerned with other cultures, particularly with English history'.[9] He holds *King Lear* up as an example of a 'life-enhancing' text, one which underlines what he considers to be the failure of the characters in the Roman plays: 'They do not learn, they do not truly suffer, they do not repent, they cannot utter sentiments of human communality' (p. 18).

I have occasionally in this book tried to argue that this need to turn the Shakespeare text to this particular purpose — one which demonstrates and, it is asserted, facilitates processes such as the acquisition of 'humility', 'growth', the understanding that the 'characters' too need to 'learn' — is an essential trait in traditional South African Shakespeare criticism. Although the subject requires far more extensive attention than can be given here it is worth reflecting upon this tendency for a moment.

Before 1960 South Africa was part of the British Commonwealth. As an erstwhile colony it was still very much perceived by English-affiliated South Africans as a non-metropolitan outpost on the periphery of the vast British empire. This mental set survived, even after the British empire itself began to decline, well beyond 1960. Literary critics, especially many of those who left Britain to come to South Africa saw themselves therefore as bearers of 'high culture' to the African subcontinent. Furthermore, after 1948 their struggle was not simply that of an English group within the dominant order which longed for connection with the 'mother country', which saw itself as an outpost of that imperial culture, and which came into daily contact with subordinate orders imbued with alien, and what is defined therefore as inferior, cultures. It was also a struggle with the emergence of a new Calvinist power group within the dominant order, one that increasingly asserted its own hegemony.

The bearers of British 'civility' now felt doubly under attack, within the dominant order as well as in confrontation with the alien cultures of the subordinate orders. With the break with the British Commonwealth in 1960 this reaction appears to have intensified. Interestingly it was then that the emergence of South African literary journals began to gather steam.

Such factors may account in part for the strident emphasis in South African literary criticism upon the need for a sense of order, growth, traditional values, now perceived presumably not only as a means of upliftment but more crucially as a means to self-protection , defence, and especially, as the survival line to the metropolis. In a world of 'racism' as well as 'savagism' in which their own participation in the existing relationships of domination and subordination is totally ignored, such literary critics turn to the Shakespeare text as a refuge and a retreat. Hence the desiccated version of their approach although they claim all the while its affinities with traditional Anglo-American criticism. In practice, however, only a highly selective kind of attention to the text is permissible, becomes in short, worth a first. Such attention often *avoids* close scrutiny of the text, and even within traditionalist frameworks, too much attention to context. These activities might reveal complexity and problem within the text where this highly selective kind of attention has a strong teleological thrust towards the discovery of points of *solution* — growth, learning, humility, that which *enables* — on the grounds of its alleged connection to 'universal' standards of value and excellence. This gives essential sustenance in what is experienced as an alien and inferior world.

Such an activity is particularly striking when applied to *King Lear,* and disturbingly so, since the play seems especially engaged with a problem of compelling interest to South African audiences: the connection between possession of land, property, and power. South Africans do not of course live in late feudal, early capitalist, early seventeenth-century

England. But fleeting reference to our own semi-industrialised modern history graphically illustrates the importance of this connection.

The Land Act of 1913 was one of the crucial pieces of legislation in the formation of what subsequently became the apartheid state. It distinguished different groups within the population of South Africa and purported to divide the land between them. In fact, as political commentators have underlined, it was to reserve less than ten per cent of the total land surface of what was then the Union of South Africa for the black inhabitants of the country. Thus the Act, in responding to the demands of white farmers to convert sharecroppers on their land into farm labourers or servants, dispossessed many black landowners and out-lawed, as well, leasing or tenant farming.

Commentators recognise that this Act, together with other laws ostensibly protecting black rights, actually eroded them. It destroyed

a whole class of peasant producers, forcing them into already crowded reserves or driving them into new and arduous social relationships — as farm workers, as mine labourers, and later in the least skilled and most badly paid positions in urban industrial, municipal and domestic employment.[10]

Perhaps the most famous of the individual reactions to this Act was from Sol T. Plaatje. He recognised the extent to which loss of land ownership and land tenancy would lead to complete political subjugation. Shortly after the passing of the Act he wrote:

. . . it will only be a matter of time before we have a Natives' Urban Act enforced throughout South Africa. Then we will have the banner of slavery fully unfurled (of course, under another name) throughout the length and breadth of the land.[11]

Other commentators then and since have recorded the reaction to the passing of the Act by large numbers of the affected population. Thus Bessie Head writes that 'rather than lose their last shred of independence . . . black people, tenants on the land, took to the road with their dying stock.'[12] Plaatje describes in detail the subsequent misery and hardship thousands of old as well as young people experienced along the open road because of their refusal to stay on the now white-owned farms as servants.[13]

The Land Act was, therefore, one of the crucially enabling laws for the subsequent system of economic exploitation and subjugation that for most of the twentieth century has characterised the experience of the inhabitants of South Africa. Moreover, the reaction of many of the dispossessed to this move, described by Bessie Head and Plaatje, is also of interest. It identifies not merely political vulnerability but bespeaks, too, an attitude, at least, of resistance to the invitation, which was made in the course of this deprivation of freedom as well as land, to servitude.

Historians working on late feudal, early capitalist England emphasise the importance of land — G.R. Elton observes that in the seventeenth-century English world, the 'economic centre of gravity' was land.[14] Moreover, significantly for *King Lear*, he stresses the extent to which possession of status was dependant upon possession of land. Seventeenth-century English society, he says

regarded only land and landed wealth as ultimately acceptable in creating status. True, there was wealth of other kinds ... mercantile and banking fortunes ... lawyers' incomes ... but the only form of wealth which could gain you social recognition was land, possession of land (p. 340).

It may perhaps be a truism to observe about *King Lear* that the King is separated from his land in order that the meaning of his status, without possession of that land, may be examined. But the importance of this in terms of economic reality and existing relations of domination and subordination has recently been particularly stressed by Jonathan Dollimore.[15] He argues that the play 'makes visible social process and its forms of ideological misrecognition' (p. 191), identifying the crucial extent to which issues of power in the play are intimately related to the question of land and material possession. Lear's use of a map at the start, his lengthy description of the nature of the territory he awards to each daughter and his mode of rewarding their love all show that he shares their value system to a significant extent. He rewards love with land — and it is this that confirms for him power and status. The manner in which he rejects Cordelia is further confirmation of the extent to which power in this society is located in possession of land and property. It is true that the attitude of France to Cordelia 'She is herself a dowry' (I. i. 241) posits an alternative vision — one in which Lear, ironically, later when he is on the heath, would like to believe pertained in his own world. But such values, it is clear, are no longer decisive in Lear's own kingdom and, when he is in power, not adhered to by Lear himself either. Dollimore describes Lear's response as king to Cordelia in this way:

Prior to Lear's disowning of Cordelia, the realities of property marriage are more or less transmuted by the language of love and generosity, the ceremony of good government. But in the act of renouncing her, Lear brutally foregrounds the imperatives of power and property relations: 'Here I disclaim all my paternal care,/Propinquity and property of blood' (I. i. 112—3; cf. ll. 196—7). Kenneth Muir glosses 'property' as 'closest blood relation' (ed. *King Lear* p. 11). Given the context of this scene it must also mean 'ownership' — father owning daughter — with brutal connotations of the master/slave relationship as in the following passage from *King John*: 'I am too high-born to be *propertied*/To be a ... serving man' (V. ii. 79—81). Even kinship then, — indeed *especially* kinship — is in-formed by the ideology of property relations, the contentious issue of primogeniture being, in this play, only its most obvious manifestation (p. 199).

Lear's retention of one hundred knights, too, as symbolic identification of his authority, confirms the materialist basis of that notion of authority. The one hundred knights prove to be the minimum 'material' possession necessary for him. Although Lear behaves under the assumption that his authority is separable from his material power, in terms of the *Oxford English Dictionary* meaning of the word 'authority' — '[the] right to enforce obedience; moral or legal supremacy; the right to command' — his retention of the knights indicates the text's recognition of the contradictions in Lear's assumptions, in the context of Jacobean society. The equally important meaning the dictionary attaches to the word 'authority', as an alternative to the 'right', is the *power* to enforce obedience. It is vital, then, to recognise that in significant ways, where his actions are concerned, Lear is as materialistic about power as those who in the course of the play displace him.

In the subsequent push Lear's daughters make to dispossess him completely and to reject his authority, Lear struggles against their attack upon his retention of the symbolic power of one hundred knights: the hundred knights stand between Lear and total dependence upon his daughters. The Fool recommends to his King:

Good Nuncle, in, ask thy daughters blessing; here's a night pities neither wise men nor Fools.

(III. ii. 13)

Lear, however, chooses the heath. When he stands there confronting the elements, he is no longer the *de facto* representative of the system of government and justice which makes its claims for hierarchy and custom.

Some critics may argue that he remains the *de jure* representative. But the play implies the ineffectuality, in Lear's society, of the myth of the Divine Right of Kings — indeed had that myth the force which James I was continually claiming for it in his own world, the text might not have shown Lear insisting with such determination upon his one hundred knights.[16] As Dollimore remarks, *King Lear* acknowledges instead that Lear's modes of implementing his power, like the modes of those who have replaced him, depend similarly upon material realities — land and property. His successors have taken over, Dollimore also emphasises, the same system. This is exactly what Edmund says — 'Well then,/Legitimate Edgar, I must have your land' (I. ii. 16). He does not wish to change the social and economic hierarchy but merely himself to inhabit it more fully. Gloucester, also, thinks as quickly of reward in terms of land and property where Edmund's loyalty is concerned, as does Cornwall.[17]

2

Recognition that power through possession of land and property is antecedent to doctrines of the Divine Right of Kings or hierarchy implies a view of the social order very different from that suggested in parts of Danby or that described by Tillyard. And in recent years numerous critics have stressed the need to treat with caution Tillyard's claim that the 'collective mind' of the people reflected unanimity of belief in traditional notions of harmony and order. Even a fairly traditional critic such as Roland Mushat Frye observes that

Ulysses' famous speech on order and degree (*Troilus* I. 3. 75—137) was taken by Tillyard as his touchstone, and we should continue to recognize its importance, but developments in the history of political thought have made such major advances since the time of Tillyard that reassessments and qualifications can and must now be made. We now know that Ulysses' eloquent words summarize an older view, that of the earlier sixteenth century, rather than that of the late Elizabethan and Jacobean periods.[18]

Such qualifications apply not merely in the realm of political thought. In the chapter on *Hamlet* I identified some of the historical antagonisms existent within the Elizabethan dominant order. As well, historians have stressed that royal power, even under Elizabeth, was limited in a number of crucial ways, although monarchs did have more or less absolute power over individuals. The monarchy could not act without parliament over matters of finance. But the parliamentarians, themselves ridden with inner rivalries and different points of view, did not approach the monarch on financial issues with much respect for her claim to rule by divine right.[19] Parliament meant trouble for the queen, which is why she avoided calling it until war forced her hand.[20] The monarchy was not only short of money but had a poor army

141

of its own.[21] Far from possessing the absolutism of its European equivalents, it was dependent in times of crisis upon the soldiers of local magnates, their retainers and tenants, and in administration its attempts at centralisation were largely undone by the fact that it had to rely upon the local gentry, who in turn gained in power and significance.[22]

The limitations of royal power, furthermore, was only one of several factors that contradict the claim that the Elizabethan and Jacobean period could have presented in its social order or in its literature a unified and consistent picture. Lawrence Stone has observed that:

whether one looks at its political support, financial resources, military and administrative power, social cohesion, legal subordination ... [or] religious unity ... [the Elizabethan polity] appears to be shot through with contradictions and weaknesses.[23]

Such problems were exacerbated under James I. G.R. Elton summarises the difficulties when James came to power in this way:

When Queen Elizabeth died, she left a system of government much debilitated by recent change. A price inflation had seriously weakened the Crown; the Church faced an insidious and fundamental attack from the Puritan party; the House of Commons had recently grown in power and independence; the ambitions of rising classes [the gentry, the bourgeoisie] were threatening the ascendancy of the monarch and aristocracy. Altogether the traditional power of the Crown was failing in the face of a variety of discontent and criticism. All these strains — which expressed themselves in a conflict between king and Commons — became increasingly obvious in the reign of James I.[24]

Moreover, Elton sees the inadequacy of the Stuart government as one of the main reasons why these many and varied problems intensified under James.

[The] early Stuart governments could not manage or persuade, because they were incompetent, sometimes corrupt, and frequently just ignorant of what was going on or needed doing ... what matters is their

142

repeated inability for reasons also often factitious, bigoted, and ill conceived to find a way through their problems (p. 161).

Of James's reign in particular, he observes that it was 'a reign which was marked even more than any other you could name in [English] history as an age in which nothing happened, in which nothing was done, in which government neglected all its duties.'[25]

Finally, it should be remembered that towards the end of Elizabeth's reign and during the beginning of James's reign the monarchy sustained a series of specific blows which Lever describes:

The rebellion of Essex and his followers, including Southampton, the patron of Shakespeare and Chapman, was followed in 1603 by the tangle of conspiracies known as the Main Plot and By-Plot, in which Cobham and Raleigh with many other noblemen were implicated. In 1605 came the Gunpowder Plot which nearly succeeded in blowing up King and Parliament together. Two years later again, in 1607, peasant disorders and riots against enclosures of the common land swept the Midland counties [including Warwickshire] to be put down by ruthless repression.[26]

None of these incidents posed any major threat to James's position on the throne but they reflect a complicated and increasingly difficult situation.

In such a context, a diversity of interpretation and understanding, rather than the existence of any unitary 'world picture' was inevitable. Even the briefest glance at the late Elizabethan and early Jacobean theatre confirms that, as much as in other contexts, in theatre too, dissent from the Tudor and Stuart official doctrines was frequent. In general Elizabethan and Jacobean audiences were used to plays which inferred or drew parallels with the current political scene, although the relatively free political comment that critics detect in Shakespeare's history plays of the 1590s was increasingly severely frowned upon. Stronger censorship, restored by James, prohibited in a number of ways any direct reference to the government.[27] Nevertheless, *King Lear* was written at a time when several plays, in one covert way or another, clearly alluded to English social relations and even to the monarch. Some of these plays, again, attracted the attention of the authorities. The detail of the lines in Jonson's *Sejanus,* which criticised the Emperor character in the play, was as applicable also to princes in general.[28] Samuel Daniel's *Philotas* (1605) appears to refer to the trial and execution of the Earl of Essex; moreover it contains 'very sharp denunciations of the arbitrary power of monarchs who tyrannise openly in despotisms, but covertly in 'free' countries like Greece — or England'.[29] During one conversation particularly, when the inevitable condemnation of the noble Philotas in a trial after torture prompts the enquiry as to why a trial of this kind is being held at all, the answer given is that 'it satisfies the world and we/Think that well done which done by law we see' to which, again, the reply is 'And yet your law but serves your private ends.'[30]

Fulke Greville's plays *Mustapha* and *Alaham,* although not meant for public performance were also identifiable as 'anti-tyrant' plays.[31] And in *The Dutch Courtesan* and *The Fawn* (1604—05), *Eastward Ho* (1605) and *The Isle of Gulls* (1606) 'James himself had been the perceived object of satire'.[32] In these and other plays, as J.W. Lever writes, 'contemporary issues constantly lurk below the surface of historical or fictitious settings' and 'for audiences of the time, the relevance was sufficiently clear'.[33] Despite the intensification of censorship Samuel Calvert could still write in 1605 that the players were performing 'the whole course of the present Time, not sparing either King, State or Religion, in so great Absurdity, and with such Liberty, that any would be afraid to hear them.'[34]

Used to numerous plays of this kind, Shakespeare's first audiences, we may be sure, would have been ready to make implicit connections between stage king, his world, and their own, when the treatment of broad issues invited this. The climate of censorship within which the theatre functioned must have positively encouraged in audience and actors alike this habit of inference.

The existence of such dissent in theatre, the range of differing attitudes, political theories or responses to which

144

this points, may help us to recognise that in *King Lear* as in many other Shakespeare texts the presence of dissenting or contradictory views is possible — at least as possible as that apparent thrust towards consolidation, or versions of it, so often discovered by South African critics. Against the continuing influence of critics such as Danby and Tillyard might be set Dollimore's reference to a distinction of Raymond Williams:

In making sense of a period in such rapid transition, and of the contradictory interpretations of that transition from within the period itself, we might have recourse to Raymond Williams's very important distinction between residual, dominant, and emergent aspects of culture (*Marxism and Literature,* pp. 121–7). Tillyard's world picture can then be seen, as in some respects a dominant ideology, in others a residual one, with one or both of these perhaps being confronted and displaced by new, emergent cultural forms ... Non-dominant elements [also] interact with the dominant forms, sometimes coexisting with, or being absorbed or even destroyed by them, but also challenging, modifying or even displacing them. Culture is not by any stretch of the imagination — not even the literary imagination — a unity.[35]

3

What strategy does the text bring into play to pursue the disturbing recognition it appears to make from the very beginning about the actual system of domination and subordination within the social order? Initially, the text offers indications to allow a tenable connection to be drawn between King Lear and James I, in the first two acts. It is important to add that this connection is not made in a reductive but in a suggestive way that might prompt reflections about the two without insistence upon a one to one equivalence.

Once the connection has been made, most likely to avoid censorship — only partly successful as we shall see in a moment — the King is removed from his position within the dominant order. The text may then proceed to explore dissenting notions about the operation of power in that order without leaving the King himself in the direct line of attack.

We need briefly to examine those details in the text which argue this. David Bevington discounts a suggestion made early in the century that King Lear is to be identified with James's own father Lord Darnley,[36] but more recently Gary Taylor provides convincing detailed evidence to show that the parallel to be made is that between King Lear and James I himself:

In electing to dramatize Lear's reign, Shakespeare was presumably paying James a compliment, for James (whose great ambition was to unite the island of Britain into one kingdom) pictured himself as the anti-type to Lear (who had divided it). But the very existence of such a perceived relationship between Lear and James opened up the possibility of other, less flattering comparisons between them.[37]

One passage in the play, in particular, which appeared in the 1608 Quarto, Taylor argues, is likely to have disappeared from the Folio edition of 1623 primarily because of political censorship initiated by Sir George Buc, Master of the Revels. It is worth examining Taylor's observations about this passage in detail because of the extent to which connections between Lear and James may be discovered in it.

In the following extract the bracketed passage appears in the Quarto but not in the Folio:[38]

Lear. A bitter foole.
Foole. Doo'st know the difference my boy, betweene a bitter foole, and a sweete foole.
Lear. No lad, teach mee.
[*Foole.* That Lord that counsail'd thee
      to giue away thy land,
  Come place him heere by mee,
      doe thou for him stand,
  The sweet and bitter foole
      will presently appeare,
  The one in motley here,
      the other found out there.
Lear. Do'st thou call mee foole boy?
Foole. All thy other Titles thou has giuen away, that thou wast borne with.
Kent. This is not altogether foole my Lord.

146

Foole. No faith, Lords and great men will not let me, if I had a monopolie out, they would haue part an't, and ladies too, they will not let me haue all the foole to my selfe, they'l be snatching;] giue me an egge Nuncle, and ile giue thee two crownes.
Lear. What two crownes shall they be?
Foole. Why, after I haue cut the egge in the middle and eate vp the meate, the two crownes of the egge.

Taylor suggests that several details in this passage brought it to the attention of the censor. For one thing the Fool's reference to monopolies towards the end of the passage has, since Dr Johnson's time, been taken to refer to James's granting of monopolies which was debated in Parliament in 1604, 1606, and again in 1610, 1614, and 1621.[39] Then Taylor suggests that the Fool's pun on 'all the foole' to mean 'all the custard' may have been a reference to the 'quite incredible competitive gluttony which had already become a notorious feature of banquets at the court of King James' (p. 103). Furthermore, 'the Fool's jibe about the king's giving away of titles ... might be interpreted as a sneer at James's wholesale dispensation of titles' (p. 103) — he 'created' more knights in the first four months of his reign than Queen Elizabeth had in the entirety of hers' (p. 103). The king's love of hunting which was widely condemned because of James's resulting neglect of his governmental duties is also clearly indicated, Taylor argues, in the whole situation:

Lear has just returned from hunting; like James when the hunting went badly, he proceeds on his arrival to upbraid and then physically attack a servant. In the passage omitted from the Folio, the Fool addresses a series of potentially objectionable remarks to a king who has given up his political responsibilities in order, apparently, to spend his time (like James) hunting (p. 104).[40]

That this passage is likely to have made so strong an identification between King Lear and James I that the censor removed it supports the contention that in the first two acts such a connection is being implied. The hints about James in the passage, from what we read about him personally, are certainly pointed. Admittedly his task as the new monarch was

147

not made easier because of his lack of personal charisma — and he had no hope of competing with the great propaganda machine that had presented 'Gloriana' to her public.[41] Again, continuing resistance to his union of the two kingdoms, Protestant unease about his toleration of and his dependence upon favourites unsuited to government added to his difficulties. His English subjects were suspicious of him despite their initial welcome and his popularity diminished even further when, to his strangeness, were added the charges of unorthodox sexual behaviour, repeated alcoholic excess, and appalling personal habits.[42] It was reported that the king always enjoyed bathing his hands in the blood of the animals he had killed in the hunt and that, when hunting, too, he 'did not dismount in order to relieve himself, and so habitually ended the day in a filthy and stinking condition'.[43] His personal behaviour, especially his love of hunting, precisely the point of criticism which Taylor identifies in the Quarto passage, argued gross neglect of his responsibilities.

But as the likely reason for the fate of this passage in the Folio demonstrates, Shakespeare was himself in danger of reprisals from the censor and if *King Lear* attends to political issues in its own world with a critical as well as an observant eye, this seems tempered on the part of the dramatist by the need for self-protection. After all, enough dramatists fell foul of Elizabethan and Jacobean censorship to encourage circumspection in all who were writing. Jonson had been imprisoned as early as 1597 for his share in *The Isle of Dogs* and he was called before the Privy Council over *Sejanus*.[44] In 1605 Marston and Chapman as well as Jonson were in prison, 'threatened with losing their ears and having their noses slit, for publishing *Eastward Ho*'.[45] Marston hid for two years as a result of the lingering threat of punishment for his part in the play. Because of the publication of *Philotas* Daniel, too, was summoned before the Privy Council in 1605, whilst Day had to defend himself in the Star Chamber over the *Isle of Gulls* (1605—06).[46]

Having introduced certain parallels between Lear and James in the first two acts and having identified, from the start of the play, the significant connection between land and power in this world, the text presents the removal of King Lear from the ruling class so that it may submit elements in the behaviour of that class to even closer scrutiny. Moreover, if the text in certain of its parallels in the first two acts implies criticism of James, this is balanced by other factors which, by the time the King has been removed from the ruling class of which he has been the centre, encourage in the audience an increasingly sympathetic attitude. Thus the mistake which Lear commits at the beginning of the play is presented as the result of faulty perception and not the consequence of the conscious self-interest displayed by Edmund, Goneril and Regan. Lear, furthermore, gains insight into the nature of his treatment of Cordelia by the end of Act I; his later understandings in terms of those around him and his view of himself may be seen as amplification of this realisation. Indeed, by the end of the second act the impulse to criticise Lear is eclipsed in the text by the presence of language that directs the audience to recognition of the enormity of what is done to him. Kent, who was not slow to criticise the King earlier, at the start of Act III, recognises the 'hard rein' (III. i. 27) which the King's daughters 'have borne/Against the old kind King' (III. i. 28) and acknowledges that of 'unnatural and bemadding sorrow/The King hath cause to plain', (III. i. 39) while Lear himself asserts 'I am a man/More sinn'd against than sinning' (III. ii. 60). Lear's questioning from Act II on, and his refusal to compromise with his daughters suggest for him a stance of resistance as well as madness — which itself was, as Maynard Mack amongst others has emphasised, a guise for social satire.[47] When he wanders on the heath, homeless and unprotected against the storm, Lear has become not merely a casualty of the ruling class, but its opponent.

In removing the ruler in this way from that position from which he normally governs, the play develops further a fairly popular dramatic convention. The technique appears in *Measure for Measure,* likely to have been written a year before. Leonard Tennenhouse has noted how, at the time of the appearance of the earlier play, a number of other well-known comedies were utilising the same device: 'a trickster figure, who is often but not always a monarch ... from ... disguise observes the state and witnesses both sexual misconduct and the abuses of political power'.[48] Tennenhouse points out that one of the effects of this technique of removing the ruler figure from his world to enable him to observe it is that 'being thus conceived as something separate from the monarch, the state and not the monarch becomes the object to which our attention is turned' (p. 141). The Duke's deputies have his authority and they represent his rule. In the same way, *King Lear* ensures that those who remain in control when Lear has been removed from power, retain the aura of legitimacy. Through the vehicle of the behaviour of Edmund, Goneril and Regan (and *not* through the presence of the one dramatic character who suggests the English king himself) the text may safely pose problems about the operation of state within the dominant order. If challenged Shakespeare might well have been able to defend himself because of this device, arguing that he was attacking not his monarch, but alarming tendencies to be identified in the state administration. And the existence of other plays adopting a similar technique would have assisted this argument.

However, although there are similarities in the removal of Lear from his world and the removal of the ruler figures from their positions of power in these other plays, similarities which might have conditioned the Shakespeare audience and censor not to rush decisively to any negative conclusions about the play's implications for the English monarch himself, Lear, unlike the Duke, does not return to power at the end.[49] Moreover the subversive implications in *King Lear* are also in their thrust more oppositional and ambiguous than those in earlier plays. It is to the reasons for this difference that we must now turn more directly.

4

If *King Lear* recognises the connection between possession of land and property and power, it also identifies the antecedence of power to justice. For this, the image of old age with which the play begins proves especially appropriate — old age, with its suggestion of the need for love, its intractability, and its fallibility presents an image of vulnerability. But when Regan says to Lear, 'I pray you, father, being weak, seem so' (II. iv. 203) she voices a different demand. A great divide opens at once between those who from the beginning of the play are indifferent and cruel towards this condition in human experience, and those who offer throughout a more compassionate response. As critics have pointed out, the capacity of men and women to act with cruelty, which this issue of old age precipitates, is attended to in the play in ways that emphasise the interconnection between individual, familial and political being — Lear as man, father, king.

Lear himself identifies the issues of power and justice which this scrutiny of cruelty raises, at first by pointing to traditional values, those values which, in turn, suggest traditionalist state ideology. On the subject of human need he tells his daughters:

> O! reason not the need; our basest beggars
> Are in the poorest thing superfluous:
> Allow not nature more than nature needs,
> Man's life is cheap as beast's.
>
> (II. iv. 269)

The king postulates here that pattern of hierarchy and order of which the monarchy itself was supposed to be the central, ideal emblem. He claims that external power and material possession are, or ought to reflect, evidence of an internal, ordered, 'essence' of man (and king) which separates him from beast. At this stage he postulates the view that human need is not simply a matter of reason and externals, maintaining that externals are important only so long as they identify 'inner worth'. He still clings, moreover, to another related traditional notion, that dress and material possessions will denote rank and quality. These were ideas, it might be said, which were used by the seventeenth-century state to legitimate its authority. In their emphasis upon such a vision of man, moreover, they postulate a being for him that is

151

somehow separate and independent of the social and economic forces in which he is situated. But we should recall that the attention given to land at the beginning of the play and the implications that flow from this have already questioned this traditional assumption.

When Lear is on the heath he begins to focus upon the problem of hidden injustice, and in so doing his language recognises that state power may well operate, in fact, in ways that are unaffected by and unrelated to notions of hierarchy and the Divine Right of Kings. He realises that power, possession of land and property do not necessarily denote morality: the externals may present a semblance of order beneath which lies criminality. 'Let the great Gods,' he cries,

> That keep this dreadful pudder o'er our heads,
> Find out their enemies now. Tremble, thou wretch,
> That hast within thee undivulged crimes,
> Unwhipp'd of Justice; hide thee, thou bloody hand,
> Thou perjur'd, and thou simular of virtue
> That art incestuous; caitiff, to pieces shake,
> That under covert and convenient seeming
> Has practis'd on man's life; close pent-up guilts,
> Rive your concealing continents, and cry
> These dreadful summoners grace
>
> (III. ii. 59)

It is true that in his recognition of 'undivulged crimes', perjurers, the 'simular of virtue', the state of hidden sinfulness, Lear participates in a long established tradition of moral or religious satire. But the dissimulation of his daughters has had political as well as familial consequences of which he, the former ruler, is now the casualty. If the father was thrust out the ruler lost power; moreover, these particular simulars of virtue remain 'unwhipped of justice' and in power, whilst Lear can only recognise their hypocrisy from a position of powerlessness. They are not merely equivocal daughters but equivocal rulers — as Kent a moment later stresses when he resolves to return to their 'house' which he sees as 'More harder than the stones whereof 'tis rais'd' (III. ii. 64). Their possession of land and property and the attendant power this

152

gives them, makes them apparently unassailable. Moreover they inhabit a system which merely *continues to operate*, using traditionalist claims to order and justice (which act as legitimations of their authority) to do so.

This identification of the hidden injustice and exploitative nature of state power is developed in the text in the presentation of the Fool and Poor Tom. Thus, as critics note, the Fool's language not only points to realisations within Lear's own mind, but also in half-forgotten old ballads and child-like inversions it directs the audience's attention to disorder and to human vulnerability in a world given to the expedient and the exploitative. In such a context, 'the codpiece that will house/Before the head has any' is doomed; in fact, 'the head and he shall louse;/So beggars marry many' (III. ii. 30). Poor Tom is primarily a victim, not of general vicissitude, but of the determined and successful thrust for power undertaken by Edmund. Exiled from the power group and a fugitive he is hunted, as Gloucester determines, by the mechanisms of state:

> All ports I'll bar; the villain shall not 'scape;
> The Duke must grant me that: besides his picture
> I will send far and near, that all the kingdom
> May have due note of him;
>
> (II. i. 83)

The behaviour of the dominant class has in effect redefined him as 'masterless', worthy of persecution, subhuman and his language, together with the image he presents in 'penury', 'filth' and with 'presented nakedness' outfacing 'the winds and persecutions of the sky' (II. iii. 12), registers the consequences. He is the Poor Tom that

> eats the swimming frog, the toad, the todpole, the wall-newt, and the water; that in the fury of his heart . . . eats cow-dung for sallets; swallows the old rat and the ditch-dog; drinks the green mantle of the standing pool;
>
> (III. iv. 137)

It is no accident that Edgar speaks these lines just after the entrance of his father who, albeit partly unwittingly, is responsible for his predicament, and who still remains, although increasingly ambiguously, a member of the dominant order. Poor Tom identifies also that punitive impulse in the dominant order to assert its authority against those whom it has created as its enemies, who are indifferently 'whipp'd from tithing to tithing, and stock punish'd, and imprison'd' (III. iv. 139). Both the Fool and Poor Tom in their situations and physical presence provide in the play persisting images of suffering at the hands of political persecution even as their language identifies an unjust and exploitative social order.

The text's identification of the cruelty of the dominant class reaches its climax in the final two scenes of Act III. Firstly, in Act III scene vi, Lear still speaks as if 'absolute justice', a notion of intrinsic justice that is separable from the social and economic conditions in which it operates, were possible. He resorts in his fantasy to a court that might try his daughters, investing each of his companions with symbolic roles derived from the traditional practice of justice:

> Bring in their evidence,
> [*To Edgar*] Thou robed man of justice, take thy place;
> [*To the Fool*] And thou, his yoke-fellow of equity,
> Bench by his side. [*To Kent*] You are o' th' commission,
> Sit you too.
>
> (III. vi. 40)

But for his robed justice, Lear chooses the fugitive from the law, Edgar; for the voice of equity, his fool; and for the commission of justice, Kent, his own exiled follower who has returned as a 'plain' man in disguise. Edgar's poignant reply to Lear 'Let us deal justly', Lear's language as it lunges out in fantasy to catch those who have seized the institutions and forms of judicial procedure:

> Stop her there! Arms, arms, sword, fire! Corruption in the place!
> False justicer, why hast thou let her 'scape?
>
> (IV. vi. 56)

and Edgar's yearning for a providential outcome at the end
of the scene

> Mark the high noises, and thyself bewray
> When false opinion, whose wrong thoughts defile thee,
> In thy just proof repeals and reconciles thee
>
> (III. vi. 116)

all communicate a longing for a potent system of 'absolute'
justice that might eradicate the present cruelty of those
who rule. This is a cruelty most famously identified in
Lear's cry:

> Then let them anatomize Regan, see what breeds about her heart. Is
> there any cause in nature that make these hard hearts?
>
> (III. vi. 79)

But set against the operation of the dominant power and
what it has chosen to define as justice, what Lear perceives to
be 'absolute justice' is no more than the practice of madmen
and fools — the outcasts of society.

In the final scene of Act III, the text literally demonstrates, against this desperate vision of 'absolute justice', the
extent to which the dominant class may operate 'lawlessly' to
preserve its position. Cornwall utters his ruthless lines

> Go seek the traitor Gloucester,
> Pinion him like a thief, bring him before us,
> [*Exeunt other servants*]
> Though well we may not pass upon his life
> Without the form of justice, yet our power
> Shall do a court'sy to our wrath, which men
> May blame but not control
>
> (III. vii. 27)

and this is followed by the putting out of the Duke's eyes *on
stage*. Like Cornwall's language this act of violence confirms
the existence of a dominant class — dominant because of its
possession of land and property — that is prepared to preserve its own position within the social order in any way
necessary. It responds to opposition with cruel indifference

and also, not merely by adapting the mechanisms of the institutions within which it works to its own purposes, but, when required, with brute force. In this scene Gloucester too cries out for a form of absolute or providential justice, for 'winged vengeance' (III. vii. 65) and also for his own forgiveness. But equally, these cries have no effect upon the situation: on the contrary by the end of the scene the ruling class merely redefines — a tactic already identified in Poor Tom's language — Gloucester's particular position as now masterless and therefore subhuman. 'Let him' says Regan, 'smell' (III. vii. 92) his way to Dover.

This recognition about the operation of state power, the language and situation that point, more especially, to the cruelty enacted upon men and women by it, strikes a chord that, like war or violence, recurs, although each time in particular and specific ways, at different moments in history. Poets in South Africa, notably in the sixties and after, react in a parallel way to the nature and impact of the dominant order, in possession of land, property and power, upon those whom it subordinates and exploits. Mazisi Kunene writes for instance of migrant workers:

> I saw them whose heads were shaved,
> Whose fingers were sharpened, who wore shoes,
> Whose eyes stared with coins.
> I saw them
> In their long processions
> Rushing to worship images of steel . . .
> There were no more people,
> There were no more women,
> Love was for sale in the wide streets
> Spilling from bottles like gold dust,
> They bought it for the festival of iron.
> Those who dug it
> Curled on the stones
> Where they died in the whirlwind.
> I saw the worshippers of iron
> Who do not speak.[50]

And Chris van Wyk, in lines which, during the crisis years of the late eighties, seem ever more powerfully to identify an impulse in the agents of the dominant class parallel to that evident in Cornwall's lines in Act III scene vii, observes:

> The sun has gone down
> with the last doused flame.
> Tonight's last bullet
> has singed the day's last victim
> an hour ago.
> It is time to go home.
>
> The hippo crawls
> in a desultory air of trimph
> through, around fluttering
> shirts and shoes full of death.
> Teargas is simmering.
> Tears have been dried by heat
> or cooled by death.
> Buckshot fills the space
> between the maimed and the mourners.
> It is time to go home.
>
> A black man surrenders
> a stolen bottle of brandy
> scurries away with his life
> in his hands.
> The policeman rests the oasis
> on his lips
> wipes his mouth on a camouflaged
> cuff.
> It is time to go home.
>
> Tonight he'll shed his uniform.
> Put on his pyjamas.
> Play with his children.
> Make love to his wife.
> Tomorrow is pay-day.
> But it is time to go home now,
> It is time to go home.[51]

5

To recognise this thrust in the play is not necessarily to suggest that *King Lear* is primarily subversive. As this chapter has already suggested, practical considerations about censorship — to go no further — would have made this unlikely. Moreover, Lear's tormented but unsuccessful search for a means of attaining 'absolute' justice and the increasing recognition the text makes that justice is not antecedent to power and property are set in Act III, frequently, beside language and situation that point to more traditional positions suggesting Christian discourse. Lear, still reeling from his growing realisation about the implications of his daughters' behaviour, repeatedly attempts to derive comfort, consolation, and even strength from the view of man as a naked suffering being. Thus his sudden remark to the Fool

> My wits begin to turn.
> Come on, my boy. How dost, my boy? Art cold?
> I am cold myself.
>
> (III. ii. 69)

posits the frailty of man and points as well to that care and compassion demonstrably lacking in the nature of the ruling power he has only a moment ago identified.

Essential humanity, the implication is, resides in that heart that can not only grieve itself, but also sorrow for a cold and suffering Fool. Lear also universalises his predicament when he sees Poor Tom:

Thou wert better in a grave than to answer with thy uncover'd body this extremity of the skies. Is man no more than this? Consider him well. Thou ow'st the worm no silk, the beast no hide, the sheep no wool, the cat no perfume. Ha! here's three on 's are sophisticated; thou art the thing itself; unaccommodated man is no more but such a poor, bare, forked animal as thou art. Off, off, you lendings! Come; unbutton here.

(III. iv. 112)

In such comments, as has often been pointed out, Lear recognises man's essence no longer, as he did earlier at the end of Act II, as residing in clothing and that which he argues clothing should represent, but in man's naked, suffering flesh.

Furthermore, in Act IV, as critics also observe, much of the language and situation communicates a powerful Christian emphasis. Thus it may be true that the act commences with Edgar's attempt at neo-stoicism, undercut at once by the entrance of his blind father. But the forgiving care of the son for the father who has oppressed him and who is now suicidal, ends positively — 'Why I do trifle thus with his despair' Edgar tells his audience, 'Is done to cure it' (IV. vi. 34). He succeeds when his father says 'henceforth I'll bear/ Affliction till it do cry out itself/"Enough, enough," and die' (IV. vi. 77). Similarly the forgiving care of the daughter for her father, the 'holy water from her heavenly eyes' (IV. iii. 31) bespeaks values of kindness and forgiveness entirely lacking in her sisters. The possibility of providential intervention also manifests itself in the language of this act, in the reaction of Albany to Regan, in the news of Cornwall's death and in Albany's hopeful cry 'This shows you are above,/You justicers, that these our nether crimes/So speedily can venge!' (IV. ii. 80). The image of the naked suffering flesh to which Lear intermittently turns in the third act recurs in the encounter between Gloucester and Lear on the beach, most powerfully perhaps in Lear's apparent understanding of his own 'humanity' when, to Gloucester's impulse to recognise his king and show his allegiance and love by kissing his hand, Lear replies 'Let me wipe it first; it smells of mortality' (IV. vi. 135). This movement towards reconciliation and Christian restoration reaches poetic culmination in the last scene of Act IV, during the climactic encounter between Cordelia and her father, in the currents of love and grief that pass between them, in the moment when the father kneels to this daughter, acknowledging his fallibility — 'a very foolish fond old man' (IV. vii. 60) — to ask her forgiveness. Such language and situation contrast powerfully with the political cruelty that has been the cumulative concern of the first three acts in particular.

6

Nevertheless the poetic and dramatic intensity of this aspect of the play does not, as Dollimore and others point out, lead to the recuperation and recovery which it seems to promise. It is lodged all the time within circumstances and language that confirm the powerlessness of such values or responses really to inform let alone alter the dominant social order.

The play recognises clearly the inadequacy of such views in a world determined by the primacy of possession of land, property and power: from the beginning, issues involving power have been increasingly identified as separate from those values that are given so poignant an emphasis especially in Acts III and IV. As the play unfolds, the state power and that of its agents continues to determine the fate of these refugees from its wrath. Thus, in Act IV, Poor Tom and the blind Gloucester whom he helps remain political refugees. Those lusts Tom claims to lie within him are at least equally powerfully present in the ruling class which has rendered himself and his father wretched. Nor will the civil war be won by the daughter who most exemplifies in her response to her father the traditional Christian virtues.

The readiness of the dominant order not merely to coerce but, when faced with difference that cannot be contained, to create subversion in order also to destroy that difference is a further recognition in the play that brings into question any suggestion at its end of recovery and consolidation. The obvious illustration of this is not simply the putting out of Gloucester's eyes, nor even Regan's sustained thrust later, in Act IV — the old man should have been eliminated, she opines, for the blinding of his eyes, she calculates, will increase resistance against the dominant order: 'where he arrives he moves/All hearts against us' (IV. v. 11). In that scene, too, her response to the 'subversive' appeal he now has remains determined: 'If you do chance to hear of that blind traitor,/Preferment falls on him that cuts him off' (IV. v. 38).

But much earlier in the play Gloucester's own response to an allegedly traitorous son — whom the audience knows to be innocent — has been no less severe. The particular circumstances he describes when he makes his 'discovery' are pertinent:

Love cools, friendship falls off, brothers divide: in cities, mutinies; in countries, discord; in palaces, treason; and the bond crack'd 'twixt son and father. This villain of mine comes under the prediction; there's son against father: the King falls from bias of nature; there's father against child. We have seen the best of our time: machinations, hollowness, treachery, and all ruinous disorders follow us disquietly to our graves. Find out this villain, Edmund; it shall lose thee nothing: do it carefully. And the noble and true-hearted Kent banish'd! his offence, honesty! 'Tis strange.

(I. ii.123)

It appears from what Gloucester registers here that his urge to punish and so preserve or display authority in a situation for multiple reasons confused, proves as important as any need for accuracy of judgement; indeed as he turns swiftly upon Edgar, the audience has already been carefully primed to see his action as a clear instance of the misapplication of justice and a misapplication of those punitive measures at the disposal of authority. Moreover, it is precisely at this point that Gloucester recalls the King's behaviour in the previous scene. Cordelia's failure to use the code her father demanded, her emphasis instead upon (significantly) the contractual nature of her relationship with him, prompted the King to make an example of her — in his case, too, anger led swiftly to fierce rejection and punishment. Furthermore Lear's reaction to Kent equally ignored the honest motives in his loyal servant's cause.

For the audience the King's response, together with Gloucester's, demonstrates misuse of power. It suggests how, in contexts of change or uncertainty, power may move swiftly, ignoring its own complicity in, or production of, disorder. We may think here of Lear's own culpability in his treatment of Cordelia and Kent, Gloucester's casual promiscuity, the implicit responsibility of these two powerful members of the dominant order for a society apparently in mutiny, discord and treason. But confronted by difference, power creates its enemies in order to assert, through punishment, its own authority. Thus Cordelia is deprived of her inheritance, Kent is banished, Edgar becomes the outlawed target of state oppression and persecution. Through such persecution too, the power of the ruling classes is entrenched. Such instances are as disturbingly interrogative of the dominant order as the image of Kent in the stocks later emblematically suggests, or as Regan's readiness to eliminate Gloucester blatantly illustrates. It is worth observing here, in the context of the present turbulence in South Africa that the government (and the classes it represents), primarily responsible for the misery and suffering in the state, nevertheless often denies this whilst reacting punitively against a wide range of individuals it chooses to redefine as subversive and worthy of severe punishment.

The demystification of authority uttered by Lear in Act IV scene vi is another way in which any apparent thrust to consolidate state power in the play is at the same time undermined. The sequence begins with a wild passage on justice spoken by the King (IV. vi. 110—34) in which his deranged mind veers from a vision of human sinfulness and the impulse to punish this to a supra-human notion of forgiveness and then to visions of human corruption and detestation. This itself is interesting in terms of the situation it evokes. The mad monarch wishing to regain control, resorts in his wildness to the demonisation of human sexuality. But we may recall briefly that if Lear's opening passage in the sequence suggests madness, this was, as I noted in the chapter on *Hamlet*, as well as earlier in this chapter, one of the guises for satire. Webster, too, situates one of his most concentrated attacks upon the entire machinery of government in his day in a lunatic asylum.[52]

The satiric and critical impulse intensifies in the passage demystifying authority that follows, even though it is balanced, significantly enough, against language that points to traditional Christian discourse placed immediately before and immediately after it — the exchange between Gloucester and Lear which recognises man as a 'ruin'd piece of Nature' (IV. vi. 136) and the moving clarity of Lear's recognition of his loyal follower:

> If thou wilt weep my fortunes, take my eyes;
> I know thee well enough; thy name is Gloucester;
> Thou must be patient; we came crying hither:
> Thou know'st the first time that we smell the air
> We wawl and cry.
>
> (IV. vi. 182)

In between these recognitions, however, of the authority of that dominant order of which until shortly before he was the most central and powerful part, Lear says:

A man may see how this world goes with no eyes. Look with thine ears: see how yond justice rails upon yond simple thief. Hark, in thine ear: change places, and, handy-dandy, which is the justice, which is the thief? Thou hast seen a farmer's dog bark at a beggar?
. . . .
> And the creature run from the cur? There thou might'st behold
> The great image of Authority:
> A dog's obey'd in office.
> Thou rascal beadle, hold thy bloody hand!
> Why dost thou lash that whore? Strip thine own back;
> Thou hotly lusts to use her in that kind
> For which thou whipp'st her. The userer hangs the cozener.
> Thorough tatter'd clothes small vices do appear;
> Robes and furr'd gowns hide all. Plate sin with gold,
> And the strong lance of justice hurtless breaks;
> Arm it in rags, a pigmy's straw does pierce it.
>
> (IV. vi. 169)

How did Shakespeare's first audience, we may wonder, with a king such as James I, respond to Lear's language, delivered insistently and compellingly in the present tense, demystifying both Authority and State Justice? James's increasingly evident personal failings, together with the negative tendencies of his administration set in the context of social and economic change must surely have impinged pressingly on the minds of many of Lear's auditors.[53] Lear's language identifies a system of justice no better than organised theft, administrators no better than dogs, vice-ridden clergymen and an exploitative economic system. Moreover, the 'deranged' King recognises the materalist basis to both power and justice. Hidden corruption when plated with gold is impervious to attempts to expose it; the powerless poor by contrast are vulnerable to attack of any kind. 'Well we knew,' writes Solomon T. Plaatje of the Land Act,

that this law was as harsh as its instigators were callous ... the law received the signature of the Governor-General on June 16; was gazetted on June 19, and forthwith came into operation ... on that day Lord Gladstone signed no fewer than sixteen new Acts of Parliament — some of them being rather voluminous — while three days earlier, His Excellency signed another batch of eight, of which the bulk was beyond the capability of any mortal to read and digest in four days ... The gods are cruel ... They might have warned us that Englishmen would agree with Dutchmen to make it unlawful for black men to keep milk cows of their own ... We knew that [this law] would, if passed, render many poor people homeless, but it must be confessed that we were scarcely prepared for such a rapid and widespread crash as it caused.[54]

This demystification of state ideology and power in *King Lear* extends, furthermore, to apparent recognition of the impact upon the poor of the sixteenth- and seventeenth-century economy, with its system of enclosures and vagrancy laws. Although here we are looking at a pre-industrial society, in South Africa we may find this detail of the Tudor and Stuart economic system of particular interest. Enclosures forced tenant farmers from the land so that the gentry could claim it for sheep and later agricultural farming. The subsequent displacement of the poor increased the already serious problem of poverty and hardship, caused too in Shakespeare's day by poor harvests, the aftermath of war, and the population explosion.[55] There was a ' "savage depression of the living standard of the lower half of the population" in Shakespeare's time — a depression created by an eight hundred per cent increase in the value of land, an overall inflation rate of five hundred per cent ... and a fall in real wages by half'.[56] Moreover, the right to remain in a particular place in Tudor and Stuart England, if it was not your place of birth, depended upon service.[57] The individual had to have a

164

master or be an apprentice. Vagrancy laws enabled the gentry, when they had a full labour supply, to remove the remainder of the poor back to the villages of their birth. These villages more often than not were poverty stricken as a result of the enclosures. And enclosures, we should remember, in a rather crude way also converted a tenant labour system into a wage labour system — the latter, as the South African State knows only too well, is easier to control and much cheaper.

When Shakespeare wrote *King Lear* pressure against enclosures was building up again in the Midlands, including Warwickshire, to break out a year or so later in rioting, which, as I have already noted, was in turn brutally suppressed by the gentry. Laws to control beggars was another way in which an attempt was made to control the vagrancy which was a continued problematic consequence of flux in economic conditions. Edgar, when he joins that class persecuted and hounded by the political power group, speaks not only of the Bedlam beggars and their suffering but of that countryside through which they roam which includes low farms, poor pelting villages, sheep-cotes, and mills. The sense of the impact of the Elizabethan/Jacobean economic system upon the powerless and landless, resonates too, when Lear cries

> Poor naked wretches, whereso'er you are,
> That bide the pelting of this pitiless storm,
> How shall your houseless heads and unfed sides,
> Your loop'd and window'd raggedness, defend you
> From seasons such as these?
>
> (III. iv. 32)

The thought prompts Lear to consider the extent to which the powerful, in possession of landed property and wealth are actively indifferent to the landless subjects of their power:

> Take physic, Pomp;
> Expose thyself to feel what wretches feel,

165

That thou may'st shake the superflux to them,
And show the Heavens more just.

(III. iv. 36)

Gloucester too, as many critics note, gives his purse to Poor
Tom, recognising that distribution 'should undo excess,/
And each man have enough' (IV. i. 71). Such language does
not constitute merely an appeal to Christian charity. It
suggests serious dissent about the social and economic order
when placed in the context of the play's early recognition of
the extent to which possession of land, property and power
is antecedent to justice and of the play's concern at the extent
to which state power may operate in the interest of the
dominant order alone. This tendency to dissent in the play is,
however, held in check as we have noted by the presence of
language and situation reflecting a more traditional position.

Such a tension and the contradictions it suggests should
not be surprising. Edward Bond detects similar contradictions
when he sets the text of *King Lear* beside what we know of
Shakespeare's own life as a landowner at Stratford and his
role in the Welcombe enclosure;

Shakespeare's plays show [a] need for sanity and its political expression, justice. But how did he live? His behaviour as a property-owner
made him closer to Goneril than Lear. He supported and benefited
from the Goneril-society — with its prisons, workhouses, whipping,
starvation, mutilation, pulpit-hysteria and all the rest of it.
An example of this is his role in the Welcombe enclosure. A large
part of his income came from rents (or tithes) paid on common fields
at Welcombe near Stratford. Some important landowners wanted to
enclose these fields . . . — and there was a risk that the enclosure would
affect Shakespeare's rents. He could side either with the landowners or
with the poor who would lose their land and livelihood. He sided with
the landowners. They gave him a guarantee against loss — and this is not
a neutral document because it implies that should the people fighting
the enclosers come to him for help he would refuse it. Well, the town
did write to him for help and he did nothing. The struggle is quite well
documented and there's no record of opposition from Shakespeare . . .
Lear divided up his land at the beginning of the play, when he was
arbitrary and unjust — not when he was shouting out his truths on the
open common.[58]

166

Other writers too move at times beyond their 'traditional' positions, beyond, some critics would argue, consciousness of aspects of the superstructure to glimpse or manifest consciousness about aspects of the substructure. Here is the great Tudor chancellor and man of religion, Sir Thomas More, understanding for a moment the materialist basis underlying the ideological legitimations of the Tudor social order:

when I consider and way in my mind all these commen wealthes, which now a dayes any where do florish, so god helpe me, I can perceave nothing but a certein conspiracy of riche men procuringe theire owne commodities under the name and title of the commen wealth. They invent and devise all meanes and craftes, first how to kepe safely, without feare of lesing, that they have unjustly gathered together, and next how to hire and abuse the worke and laboure of the poore for as litle money as may be. These devises, when the riche men have decreed to be kept and observed under coloure of the comminaltie, that is to saye, also of the pore people, then they be made lawes.[59]

More's language, admittedly coincidentally, approximates descriptions of the combined onslaught of South African mining and industrial capital which culminated in the Land Act and related legislation and which led through the ensuing sixty odd years to the steady destruction of surviving pockets of black freehold throughout South Africa. His voice finds an answering call in the lament of Don Mattera for just such another conspiracy of powerful men 'procuring their own commodities under the name and title of the commonwealth' — in this case by yet another seizure of land and property:

o sophia sophiatown
you speak to me from the ashes of broken days
and from the twilight mist i hear a song rolling softly
softly rolling
a song for yesterday.[60]

Harriet Hawkins in an article entitled 'The Morality of Elizabethan Drama: Some Footnotes to Plato' coming to the plays
of the period with a rather different perspective, cautions
against that criticism which not only re-enacts conflicts in the
texts, but attempts to resolve them.[61] If we recognise, as she
puts it, the fact that Shakespeare confronts us 'with some of
the harshest truths of human experience' (p. 32) we ought
also to be able to admit that 'great poets . . . frequently
refuse to impose unreal solutions on problems inherent in our
human condition' (pp. 31—2). She quotes too the remarks of
Chekhov to a publisher critic on this point warning against
the confusion of

the solution of a problem and *the correct posing of a question.* Only
the second is obligatory for the artist. Not a single problem is solved in
Anna Karenina and in *Eugin Onegin,* but you find these works quite
satisfactory . . . because all the questions in them are correctly posed.
(p. 13)

Does *King Lear* in its final effect emerge as a text of consolidation or of subversion? Or is its final impact one of containment? Stephen Greenblatt argues that 'there are moments
in Shakespeare's career — *King Lear* is the greatest example
— in which the process of containment is strained to the
breaking point'.[62] Another critic, James Kavanagh, interestingly identifies the use the text makes of Lear the character rather than king as a vehicle for

a universal empathetic appeal; this is the position of the degraded old
man cast into the elements, victim of and witness to a world in which
cruelty and egotism reign. This aspect of Lear, echoed in the play by
Gloucester, makes sharp criticism of the anarchic world of isolated,
calculating egos that is the feudal ideology's image of a society ruled by
greed and the minds of fallen men. And the play elicits identification
with this attack on the spectre of a bourgeois ethic by reducing Lear to
common humanity, the 'unaccommodated man . . . poor, bare, forked
animal' (III. iv. 109—10) . . . This is a strikingly egalitarian move . . .[63]

But he proceeds to observe that

egalitarianism is finally more at home within bourgeois republican than within aristocratic Christian humanism, and *King Lear* appropriates egalitarianism for the latter only in order to try to occupy and *control* ... The play attempts to incorporate the strongest element of bourgeois ideology in its language and images as an unequal, dominated element of a transformed aristocratic ideology — one that is now stronger for its unprecedented unitary cast and universalized appeal, but one also now attached to a discourse which can only undermine that ideology's own legitimacy (p. 158).

... the staying power of *King Lear* and of Shakespeare's work in general, is partly a result of its fearlessness in representing and giving discursive space to such opposed ideological elements. This also destabilizes the reconciliation effect that the text seeks to achieve within a given cultural ideology (p. 159).

In this context we might glance, finally, at Dollimore and Sinfield's argument in the context of *Henry V* that

strategies of containment presuppose centrifugal tendencies, and how far any particular instance carries conviction cannot be resolved by literary criticism. If we attend to the play's different levels of signification rather than its implied containments, it becomes apparent that the question of conviction is finally a question about the diverse conditions of reception.[64]

As South Africans studying *King Lear,* in whatever way we may choose to explore the problem of exactly where the play may stand in relation to the social order of which it is part, that level of signification in the text that has seemed most pertinent to us so far is also the most appropriate place at which to conclude. We may recall that in *Measure for Measure* the argument for containment, despite the subversive tendencies that play reveals, as Tennenhouse recognises, is strong. The disguised ruler returns at the end; the glimpses of that which threatens the social order result in the ratification of the concept of hierarchy and the value of the ruler himself. But in *King Lear* the King, together with Cordelia, is dead by the end of the play. As I also remarked, despite the presence of language positing Christian values the play indicates that these are powerless against an order informed by the primacy of land, property and power. The fact that the dominant class claims these values as part of its ideology could not be more telling, as Dollimore has so cogently argued: 'Surely in *Lear*, as in most of human history, "values" are shown to be terrifyingly dependent upon whatever "large orders" actually exist; in civil war especially — which after all is what *Lear* is about — the two collapse together.'[65] And Dollimore emphasises that the 'failure of those values is in part due to the fact that they are (or were) an ideological ratification of the very power structure which eventually destroys them' (p. 193).

The final act presents the death of both daughter and father as ineluctable despite the fact that they cherish these values. It may be true that, as in *Hamlet*, in this scene, Shakespeare's concern with accident as itself a tragic and mysterious aspect of this world, the unpredictability and uncontrollability of human life, is identified. This has encouraged some critics to base their whole reading of the play upon this recognition. It might be seen as an important preoccupation of Shakespeare, resulting from his sense of an imperfect world — latent in *Julius Caesar* in the fact that neither Brutus nor Caesar can control the outcome of their respective decisions, explicit in the final scene of *Hamlet*, as I suggested in the second chapter, where the duel provides an emblematic enactment of the fact of accident in human experience, and present even in *Othello,* in the series of accidents which make Desdemona herself an active although unwitting agent in Iago's plans.

But the death of Cordelia, we must hasten to add, is not primarily the result of accident. By the end of the play, what Lear and his daughter have experienced is the result, more crucially than the factor of accident, of political oppression. Moreover, as victims of a dominant class to which they no longer belong — one which operates as it always seems to have done, in its own interest, and which uses state power and ideology to preserve its hegemony — they are now defeated in civil war, and face incarceration. Lear says to his daughter of their coming imprisonment, 'We two alone will sing like birds i' th' cage' (V. iii. 9) and his mind, broken by oppression, envisages in the context of imprisonment a child-like fantasy of escape. His language, however, is no less located in the hard context of political reality. They will talk, he says, 'of court news', of

> Who loses and who wins; who's in, who's out;
> And take upon's the mystery of things,
> As if we were Gods' spies
>
> (V. iii. 17)

But, even as his mind comes back to the fact of oppression, the state's use of control by spying (with which *Hamlet* has been so concerned), he attempts to flee again. They will be the spies of God, he dreams, possessors of an omnipotent detachment free from the pressures of polity though still, ironically, practising a form of (divine) surveillance. But, yet again, his mind returns once more, and finally, to the 'wall'd prison' around them (V.iii.18).

It is that dominant class of which Lear was once himself part that is primarily responsible for the two deaths at the play's end. When Lear re-enters the stage, we might, only in one sense fancifully, suggest that he carries not merely the innocent murdered Cordelia, but all of those, not only in Shakespeare's day, who have died similarly. This is *ostensibly* the last thrust of a power group within the dominant order, a thrust which ends with Edmund's death. In another sense the tendencies and characteristics the play has recognised continue beyond the last words of the text, in Shakespeare's own world and beyond that too. Dollimore observes in this connection that 'far from transcending in the name of an essential humanity the gulf which separates the privileged from the deprived, the play insists on it (p. 192). Lear is only able to learn anything once he has lost power totally; rulers in power, the play acknowledges, never do expose themselves to 'feel what wretches feel' (III. iv. 34) (pp. 191–2). Foregrounding of the image of Lear carrying the dead Cordelia, the image too of the powers that be, crying at the hint of danger, at the sound of an angry oppositional voice, 'shut up your doors . . . 'tis a wild night . . . come out o' th' storm' (II. iv. 311) and the image of that wild old man himself, deprived of power, realising, in part confusedly, the real nature of its operation, *all set against* the continuing indifference of that ruling class in its assertion of hegemony — more than, perhaps, the foregrounding of any other images in Shakespeare's plays — has resonance for us, here, in South Africa.

Notes

1 Arthur Sherbo ed., *The Yale Edition of the Works of Samuel Johnson, vol. VIII: Johnson on Shakespeare* (New Haven: Yale University Press, 1968), p. 703.

2 Harry Levin, *Shakespeare and the Revolution of the Times* (Oxford: Oxford University Press, 1976), p. 165.

3 All references to *King Lear* in this chapter are taken from *King Lear,* ed. Kenneth Muir (London: Methuen, 1969). References are to act, scene and line. Where more than one line is quoted, the number for the 'last' quoted line is given.

4 Levin, *Shakespeare and the Revolution of the Times,* p. 165.

5 John F. Danby, *Shakespeare's Doctrine of Nature* (London: Faber and Faber, 1975).

6 Danby's use of Hobbes depends upon work that actually appeared in the 1640s and beyond — the *Leviathan* was published in 1651, forty-six years after we believe *King Lear* to have been written. Edmund's views of nature, as critics have noted, as much as anything else suggest a libertine naturalism that distorts the relativism of Montaigne in the direction of self interest.

7 The various stages in this particular debate are summarised in Lawrence Stone, *The Causes of the English Revolution 1529–1642* (London: Routledge and Kegan Paul, 1972), pp. 26–40. Stone notes Tawney's advocacy of the rise of the gentry, his own argument about the decline of the aristocracy, and Trevor-Roper's thesis that the rising gentry were courtiers whereas the party paying the price for this rise was the country gentry. See also Stone, pp. 110–11 on social and geographic mobility during this period.

8 M.J.C. Echeruo, 'Dramatic Intensity and Shakespeare's *King Lear',* *English Studies in Africa,* 6:1, 1963, pp. 44–50. Peter Bryant in his 'Nuncle Lear', see chapter 1, note 3, also virtually ignores

Act V.

9   Geoffrey Hughes, ' "A World Elsewhere": Romanitas and its Limi-
    tations in Shakespeare', *English Studies in Africa*, 28:1, 1985,
    pp. 1–19, p. 1.

10 Tom Lodge, *Black Politics in South Africa since 1945* (Johannes-
    burg: Ravan, 1983), p. 2.

11 Sol T. Plaatje, *Native Life in South Africa* (London: P.S. King and
    Son Ltd., 1916; Johannesburg: Ravan, 1982), p. 72.

12 Bessie Head, Foreword to *Native Life in South Africa* by Sol T.
    Plaatje, p. xi.

13 Plaatje, *Native Life in South Africa*, pp. 78ff. To illustrate journal-
    istic insensitivity to what was happening, Plaatje quotes the following
    extract from *The Harrismith Chronicle, 'An Ancient Couple*: A
    venerable Native whose age is no less than 119 years, accompanied
    by his wife, aged 98, and a son who is approaching 80, left Harri-
    smith on Tuesday by train for Volksrust. The old man acquired
    some property in the Transvaal, and is leaving this district to start a
    new home with as much interest in the venture as if he were a
    stripling of twenty. The old lady had to be carried to the train, but
    the old man walked fairly firmly. The aged couple were the centre
    of much kindly attraction, and were made as comfortable as pos-
    sible for their journey by railway officials. It is difficult to realize
    in these days of rapid change that in the departure from the Free
    State of this venerable party we are losing from our midst a man
    who was born in 1794, and has lived no less than three centuries
    of time' (pp. 94–5).

14 G.R. Elton, *Studies in Tudor and Stuart Politics and Government:
    Papers and Reviews 1973–1981,* vol. III. (Cambridge: Cambridge
    University Press, 1983), p. 340.

15 Jonathan Dollimore, *Radical Tragedy* (Sussex: The Harvester
    Press, 1984), pp. 189–203. Again my indebtedness to Dollimore
    is everywhere evident in what follows although of course I alone
    am responsible for its failings.

16 Alvin B. Kernan, *'King Lear* and The Shakespearean Pageant of
    History' in *On King Lear,* ed. Lawrence Danson, (Princeton:
    Princeton University Press, 1981), pp. 7–24, has argued: 'Lear's
    band of followers, his hundred knights, directly reflects the ques-
    tion of maintenance, the rights of the old feudal barons to keep
    private armies: and Goneril's whittling away of the knights "in
    the tender of a wholesome weal" – "What need one?" – reflects
    almost equally directly the ongoing efforts of the state to eli-
    minate these riotous, dangerous, and uneconomic groups of armed

retainers, and to change the aristocracy from a military class to dependants of the crown' (pp. 11–12). If this connection is tenable it helps to underline the extent to which Lear's exchange with his daughters has a materialist basis.

17 Dollimore, *Radical Tragedy*, pp. 198, 199, 201.

18 Frye, *The Renaissance Hamlet*, p. 45.

19 G.R. Elton, *Studies in Tudor and Stuart Politics and Government: Papers and Reviews 1946–1972*, vol. II *Parliament* (Cambridge: Cambridge University Press, 1974), writes: 'It is ... time that historians cured themselves of the habit of referring to the Commons as a body, as though those more than 400 men were as single-headed and single-purposed as the king himself' (p. 159).

20 Stone, *The Causes of the English Revolution*, writes: 'With its control over taxation, especially for war, and its control over legislation, especially concerning religion [Parliament] was strategically placed ... During the course of the middle and late sixteenth century many things happened to increase Parliament's powers and to diminish the capacity of the Crown to control it' (p. 92).

21 Stone, *The Causes of the English Revolution*, pp. 60–2.

22 Stone, *The Causes of the English Revolution*, pp. 62–4.

23 Stone, *The Causes of the English Revolution*, p. 67.

24 Elton, *Studies*, vol. II, p. 157.

25 Elton, *Studies*, vol. III, p. 282.

26 J. Lever, *The Tragedy of State* (London: Methuen, 1971), pp. 3–4.

27 Margot Heinemann, *Puritanism and Theatre* (Cambridge: Cambridge University Press, 1980) notes: 'The actual censorship after 1603 was carried out on behalf of the court by the Master of the Revels (who held office under the Lord Chamberlain) ... For every prosecution that we know about, for every manuscript examined that has been cut or altered by the censor or under his direction, there must be many similar cases of which no record survives. But more important, this strict control and supervision must have been in the minds of the players and writers, who would usually accept it as one of the limitations under which they had to work ... Control and censorship on behalf of the Crown in Jacobean times was much tighter than it had been under Elizabeth. Within three or four years of his coronation James had virtually taken into royal hands the control of players, plays, dramatists and theatres' (p. 36). 'It was, of course, almost exclusively a *political* censorship. Except for the specific ban on oaths and profane language introduced in 1606, the censor was scarcely concerned with questions of morality or good taste' (p. 37). Heinemann cites

174

Wickham's comment on the exact nature of this political censorship: 'The most topical of all subject matter, the relation between Church, State and individual human being — the topic which had kept English drama so vividly in touch with life in the Tudor era — was the very material which the whole machinery of censorship and control had been devised to suppress' (p. 38).

Heinemann, we may finally note here, lists the guiding principles on which Jacobean and Caroline censors worked, as crystallised by G.E. Bentley: 'They were to forbid:

1 Critical comments on the policies or conduct of the court.
2 Unfavourable presentation of friendly foreign powers or their sovereigns, great nobles, or subjects.
3 Comment on religious controversy.
4 Profanity and oaths (from 1606 onwards).
5 Personal satire on influential people.

To these may be added a ban on the representation of any ruling sovereign, even a favourable one' (p. 39).

28 Heinemann, *Puritanism and Theatre*, pp. 39—40.
29 Heinemann, *Puritanism and Theatre*, pp. 40—1.
30 Cited in Heinemann, *Puritanism and Theatre*, p. 41.
31 Heinemann, *Puritanism and Theatre*, p. 43.
32 Gary Taylor, 'Monopolies, Show Trials, Disaster, and Invasion: *King Lear* and Censorship' in *The Division of The Kingdoms* ed. Gary Taylor and Michael Warren (Oxford: Clarendon Press, 1983), pp. 75—119, p. 105.
33 Lever, *The Tragedy of State*, p. 2.
34 Cited in Dollimore, *Radical Tragedy*, p. 23.
35 Jonathan Dollimore, 'Introduction: Shakespeare, cultural materialism and the new historicism' in *Political Shakespeare*, ed. Dollimore and Sinfield, p. 14.
36 Bevington, *Tudor Drama and Politics*, p. 24 ff.
37 Taylor, *The Division of the Kingdoms*, p. 104.
38 Taylor, *The Division of the Kingdoms*, p. 102. I have used the lines as they appear in Taylor's chapter.
39 Taylor, *The Division of the Kingdoms*, p. 102. Christopher Hill, *The Century of Revolution 1603—1714*, (Edinburgh: Thomas Nelson, 1962) writes, 'In 1601 a member of Parliament asked, when a list of monopolies was read out, "Is not bread there?" His irony exaggerated only slightly' (p. 32). Hill's list of items under monopoly extends over a full page. He remarks that by '1621 there were alleged to be 700 of them' (p. 33).
40 Taylor, *The Division of the Kingdoms*, argues: 'Any one of these

features — the abdicated king hunting, the knights, the jokes about monopolies, or courtiers, or promiscuous ladies, or bad advisers, or giving away titles — *might*, in isolation, have passed unnoticed; their conjunction, in one brief passage, even the blindest censor could hardly overlook. But even if Buc were half asleep when he first read the submitted manuscript of *King Lear*, one line alone would have been enough to wake him up: 'Do'st thou call mee foole boy?' ... James himself was by 1606 beginning to be characterised as less than astute in his managing of political affairs. He may already have been memorably epitomised as 'the wisest foole in Christendom'; but even if that witticism dates from later in the reign, it simply articulates the disparity, obvious soon enough, between James's much-vaunted learning and his relative political ineptitude.. In politics as in the theatre, the paying public relishes any demonstration that those who most boast of their own mental powers are in fact fools, and James I set himself up for such debunking. In early 1606, it would have been hard not to see the Fool's jibe at Lear as a reflection of King James's own royal fool commenting on the folly of James himself' (pp. 104—5).

41 Stephen Greenblatt, *Renaissance Self-Fashioning*, writes: 'Elizabeth's exercise of power was closely bound up with her use of fictions . . . she was a living representation of the immutable within time, a fiction of permanence. Through her, society achieved symbolic immortality and acted out the myth of a perfectly stable world, a world which replaces the flux of history . . . The gorgeous rituals of praise channeled national and religious sentiments into the worship of the prince, masked over and thus temporarily deflected deep social, political, and theological divisions in late sixteenth-century England, transformed Elizabeth's potentially disastrous sexual disadvantage into a supreme political virtue and imposed a subtle discipline upon aggressive fortune seekers' (pp. 166—9). Stone, *The Causes of the English Revolution*, pp. 88—9, describes the process of identification of Elizabeth's person with English religious nationalism. The closer this was 'the more difficult it became to pass the identification on to her successor. It was the Stuarts who had to pay the political bill for the exaltation of Elizabeth' (p. 89).

42 Stone, *The Causes of the English Revolution*, p. 89.

43 Stone, *The Causes of the English Revolution*, p. 89.

44 Heinemann, *Puritanism and Theatre*, p. 39.

45 Heinemann, *Puritanism and Theatre*, p. 43.

46 Heinemann, *Puritanism and Theatre*, pp. 40, 44.

47 Maynard Mack, 'The Jacobean Shakespeare' in *Jacobean Theatre*, ed. J.R. Brown and B. Harris, Stratford-upon-Avon Studies, (London: Edward Arnold, 1960), pp. 11—41, observes: 'both [Lear] and Hamlet can be privileged in madness to say things — Hamlet about the corruption of human nature, and Lear about the corruption of the Jacobean social system ... which Shakespeare could hardly have risked apart from this licence. Doubtless one of the anguishes of being a great artist is that you cannot tell people what they and you and your common institutions are really like ... without being dismissed as insane' (p. 39).

48 Leonard Tennenhouse, 'Representing Power: *Measure for Measure* in its Time' in *The Power of Forms in the English Renaissance*, ed. Stephen Greenblatt (USA: University of Oklahoma, 1982), pp. 139—156, p. 139.

49 In plays with disguised ruler figures, of which *Measure for Measure* seems one, Tennenhouse observes that the final aim appears authentication of the traditional hierarchy. He argues that in truth the monarch was always the object of public attention, 'constituting the court around him, in full view at all times and the single figure upon whom everyone else gazed' (p. 141). Thus Tennenhouse argues that although the play's separation of the ruler/ monarch figure and the state posits the possibility of a lack of interdependence between monarch and deputies and the prefigurement of bureaucracy, this is not the final outcome. The implication at the end of *Measure for Measure* is that only with the return of the true monarch and 'with his authority does the law cease to be arbitrary and punitive, for he alone acts out a selfless desire for the good of the state' (p. 143). Tennenhouse suggests that such plays are thus against the corruption of monarchless states and contain at least as strong an argument for centralised hierarchical government.

50 Mazisi Kunene, 'The Civilisation of Iron' in *A Century of South African Poetry*, ed. Michael Chapman (Johannesburg: Ad. Donker, 1981), p. 244.

51 Christopher van Wyk, 'A Riot Policeman' in *It Is Time To Go Home* (Johannesburg: Ad. Donker, 1979), pp. 50—1.

52 See John Webster, *The Duchess of Malfi* in *The Selected Plays of John Webster*, ed. Jonathan Dollimore and Alan Sinfield (Cambridge: Cambridge University Press, 1983), Act IV scene ii.

53 We may note here that, apart from the social and economic problems already mentioned, an intensive struggle between King, Commons, and the Bench has been identified in the early years of James's reign. Tennenhouse, 'Representing Power: *Measure for*

Measure in its Time', p. 144, writes: 'James was the first monarch to claim sovereignty according to ancient rights and privileges that gave him complete authority over Parliament. By the close of that first Parliament, some men in Commons insisted to the contrary, the King's supreme authority belonged to him only in Parliament, not when he acted alone. A third perspective was offered by Sir Edward Coke, who, speaking for the supreme authority of the common law, argued, ". . . when an act of Parliament is against common right and reason . . . the common law will control it and adjudge it to be void".'

Tennenhouse emphasises that although these various institutions of the state operated within a common belief in a centralised political model 'each competed intensely for that power, each laid special claims to that power and each positioned itself, therefore, at the top of a hierarchy' (p. 144).

54 Plaatje, *Native Life in South Africa,* pp. 81, 82, 22.

55 Stone, *The Causes of the English Revolution,* writes: 'In the sixteenth century the combination of rapidly rising food prices and stagnant rents shifted the distribution of agricultural profits away from the landlord and towards the tenant. In the early seventeenth century rents increased more rapidly than prices, and profits flowed back to the landlord and away from the tenant. This shift to economic rents was accompanied by a reorganisation of property rights, by which more and more land fell into private control through enclosures of both waste and common fields. As a result of this process and of the engrossing of farms into larger units of production, there began to emerge the tripartite pattern of later English rural society, landlord, prosperous tenant farmers, and landless labourer. These changes were essential to feed the additional mouths, but tens of thousands of small-holders were driven off the land or reduced to wage labourers while others found their economic position undermined by encroachment on, or overstocking of, the common lands by the big farmers and the landlords. The enclosure became a popular scapegoat for the dislocations inevitable in so major a redistribution and reallocation of the land, but there can be no doubt that the extra millions of Englishmen were only fed at the cost of much individual hardship suffered by many of the small peasantry' (p. 68).

56 Kernan, *'King Lear* and the Shakespearean Pageant of History', p. 11. (Kernan partly quotes Hill in this citation.) Carl Bridenbaugh, *Vexed and Troubled Englishmen 1590–1642* (Oxford: The Clarendon Press, 1968), writing on the beginnings of the

American people, observes: 'The half-century after 1590 was a time of profound, unprecedented, and often frightening social ferment for the people of England. During these years nearly every member of the lower orders in the countryside and in the towns knew deprivation and genuinely feared insecurity; and well he might, for close to a majority of the population found themselves living perilously near the level of bare subsistence . . . Englishmen were experiencing the cumulative effects of long-range, persisting disturbances inherited from previous generations to which new disorders were being constantly added' (p. 355). Christopher Hill, *The Century of Revolution*, writes: 'to contemporaries, struck by poverty and vagabondage, the overpopulation seemed absolute . . . Wage labourers did not share in the profits of industrial expansion. As prices rose during the sixteenth century, the purchasing power of wages had fallen by something like two thirds. Since the numbers of those permanently dependent on wages was increasing, the number of those on the margin of starvation was increasing too. This fall in real wages was catastrophic for those who sold or were evicted from their plots of land and became entirely dependent on earnings. The real earnings of a worker born in 1580 would never exceed half of what his great-grandfather had enjoyed. Real wages reached their lowest point in James's reign . . .' (p. 24).

Hill, *The Century of Revolution*, writes: 'The harsh Poor Law was breaking up the bands of roaming vagabonds which had terrorised Elizabethan England; but it could not prevent London attracting an underworld of casual labourers, unemployables, beggars, and criminals. The prescribed penalty of whipping home unlicensed beggars checked freedom of movement, and detained a surplus of cheap labour in many rural areas' (p. 26). Wrightson, *English Society, 1580—1660*, notes: 'Poverty, of course, was nothing new. English society had never been able to provide adequately for all its members. Yet the later sixteenth and early seventeenth centuries saw the growth of a poverty which was different in both its nature and extent from that which had been known earlier . . . By the end of the sixteenth century . . . the poor were no longer the destitute victims of misfortune or old age, but a substantial proportion of the population living in constant danger of destitution, many of them full-time waged labourers . . . The extent of the problem was frightening, though it varied . . . from area to area . . . the settled poor [were] relatively fortunate in that they had a recognised place in society and were eligible for parish relief under the Elizabethan Poor Laws. Beyond them and well outside the charitable consideration of the authorities, were the vagrant poor ... How many of them wandered the roads of the period it is impossible to say, though their numbers were undoubtedly high' (p. 141). And Hill *The Century of Revolution,* observes: 'although it would be wrong to think of any body of organised discontent, there is a permanent background of potential unrest throughout these decades. Given a crisis — a famine, large-scale unemployment, a breakdown of government — disorder might occur, as it did in 1607 when there were 'Levellers' in Northamptonshire and 'Diggers' in Warwickshire ... The prevention of peasant revolt was the monarchy's job; in this it had the support of the propertied class' (pp. 27—8).

58 Edward Bond, *Bingo* (London: Eyre Methuen, 1974), Introduction p. ix.

59 Sir Thomas More, *Utopia with the 'Dialogue of Comfort'* (London: J.M. Dent, no date), p. 112.

60 Don Mattera, 'A Song For Yesterday', *The English Academy Review,* 1983, vol. 1, p. 83.

61 Harriet Hawkins, 'The Morality of Elizabethan Drama: Some Footnotes to Plato' in *English Renaissance Studies,* ed. John Carey (Oxford: Clarendon Press, 1980), pp. 12—32, pp. 31—2.

62 Greenblatt, 'Invisible bullets: Renaissance authority and its subversion, *Henry IV and Henry V'* in *Political Shakespeare,* ed. Dollimore and Sinfield, pp. 18—45, p. 45.

63 Kavanagh, 'Shakespeare in Ideology', pp. 157—8.

64 Dollimore and Sinfield, 'History and Ideology: the instance of *Henry V',* p. 225.

65 Dollimore, *Radical Tragedy,* p. 202.

5 Towards a People's Shakespeare

Stephen Greenblatt observes in *Renaissance Self-Fashioning*:

if cultural poetics is conscious of its status as interpretation this consciousness must extend to an acceptance of the impossibility of fully
recognising and re-entering the culture of the sixteenth century, of
leaving behind one's own situation: it is everywhere evident . . . that the
questions I ask of my material and indeed the very nature of this
material are shaped by the questions I ask of myself.[1]

Those of us who opt in South Africa, in turbulent and
crucial times, to look at literature need to recognise the
importance of this observation. The South African social
formation is one characterised by deep divisions, conflict,
patterns of exploitation. Mining, industrial and agricultural
capital continue to assert dominance, while the increasing
strength and self-awareness of the working classes, the
growth of trade unionism, the thrust towards resistance,
has intensified to make virtually the whole country a site
of continuing and bitter struggle.

As teachers and students of Shakespeare we have a
particular responsibility when we take up the text.

Traditional South African criticism has chosen to describe
an idealist Shakespeare. This is one who moves away from
the social formation within which he is located and one who
seeks essential, universal and transcendant truths. These truths
are about human nature as we may perceive it through the
study of a handful of heroic individuals. In crucial respects
these individuals, when we respond in this way to them,
may reach us through time as we ourselves float away from
our own world, narcissistically, to join them. Such individuals
appear to be free of political, social, economic — even geographic — particularity. To appreciate them all we apparently
need is a certain sensibility — in the opinion of many tradi-

tionalist critics, it would appear, one sorely lacking in the vast mass of humanity — a certain instinctive feel for eternal truths about human nature. In this endeavour a crude or simplistic form of psychologising is permissible but, again, this must be of a very instinctive and especially non-psycho-analytic kind. Most requisite, perhaps, is the conviction, held with an arrogant as well as a religious fervour, that the text, like the Bible, can become for those few readers with the right sensibility, a means of self-improvement, growth, private moral awareness. In this way too, the text becomes for the reader a means of distinguishing favourably his own personal powers of discrimination from a world of the insensible, or worse, the non-literate.

We may be sure that this traditional criticism which remains powerful in many South African educational institutions, will, even if belatedly, increasingly incorporate, say, certain structuralist or deconstructionist tactics. This will always be with results of the most depoliticised kind.

Such a use made of the Shakespeare text is demonstrably convenient to the South African state apparatus. Shakespeare continues to be taught widely in South African universities and schools, and continues to feature hugely on Department of Education and Training syllabuses as well as on provincial education department or the Joint Matriculation Board syllabuses. Similarly, it is the state-controlled theatre organisations, particularly, which continue to produce his plays.

The students who pass through these institutions and the lecturers and teachers who emerge from them will, in turn, themselves be responsible for the educative process in the South Africa of the future. In the teaching or study of Shakespeare, unless we are willing at a profound level to countenance a shift in emphasis, away from the determinedly simplistic view of traditional approaches — desiccated echoes of the Anglo-American approaches on which they are modelled — we shall continue to help *apartheid*. We will produce students who, in their experience of the Shakespeare text will have had all their tendencies towards submission to prevailing relationships of domination and subordination encouraged.

We must therefore, in both the study and teaching of Shakespeare, endeavour to admit not only the broader Anglo-American traditions, but also those levels of signification in the Shakespeare text that themselves indicate conditions of material struggle.

The plays likely to have been written in the period 1601—1606 are of particular interest to a South African audience. They emerge during a period of great change in British history. There was the movement from a feudal to an early capitalist state. During this period Queen Elizabeth died amidst feelings of insecurity about her successor, James I, a far less able monarch. Moreover, historians trace within the Elizabethan and the Jacobean social formation struggles and divisions that were to intensify over the next two or three decades and lead to civil war.

Side by side with the impulse towards the assertion of traditional values, each text I have examined in this book suggests, in different ways, uncertainty and unease. In *Hamlet,* likely to have been written in 1601, we have seen how the text partly portrays the operation of power by drawing upon Christian discourse, and upon notions of hierarchy and custom. Yet despite the presence of this discourse or the attempt to understand events in terms of the notions of accident and mystery, the play also portrays a dominant class that is riven with inner conflict and that operates, in order to preserve itself, in ways that are often indifferent to notions of hierarchy or Christianity.

Othello, thought to have been written three years later, appears when an untested new monarch, James I, has ascended the throne. The new king not only inherited great problems which were exacerbated in the last years of Elizabeth's reign, but he was also less impressive, both personally and as an administrator. *Othello*, even more than *Hamlet*, suggests unease about the operation of power. Again, there is evidence of traditional discourse in the text: about the nature of both judgement and perception in a fallen world, about the problems of appearance and reality, and about the vulnerability, to the socially destructive, of those who adhere to values based upon hierarchy and Christianity. But the play is also disturbingly interrogative about the dominant classes and their use of the judicial and administrative apparatus. By means partly of the colonial location, the text examines the potential within the ruling classes for the manipulation of judicial procedure and narrative to abuse and dominate — the extent, moreover, to which the ruling class is itself torn with inner division and violence.[2]

The disturbing recognitions about power made in *Hamlet* and *Othello* are developed in *King Lear,* which is likely to have appeared a year later in 1605. The text evidences certain strategies of self-protection against censorship; but given this, it scrutinises directly the capacity of the dominant classes for cruelty and the continued acquisition of wealth, land and property in the assertion of power. This, we may note, is only one short step and a year away from the presentation in *Macbeth* of an equivocal ruler directly on stage. The Scottish king who in that text is so different from the English king, is nevertheless played before an audience that has in it an English king who is too, the Scottish king. Again the equivocal nature of power, especially in a time of great change — the seed of which is planted much earlier and repeatedly grappled with in these and other Shakespeare plays — we in South Africa recognise and increasingly understand only too well.

Those of us who seek an equitable, just and democratic South Africa, working as we must within existing institutions, need to recognise that there is no neutral territory for Shakespeare studies in present-day South Africa. If this book will have any value at all it will be as a first step in the struggle to wrest the Shakespeare text from the conservative grasp of traditionalist critics. We need to work for the development of readings of the texts that will free them from ruling class appropriation, from their present function as instruments of hegemony. In so doing we may pave the way for a new educational dispensation, a dispensation that will include one day, amongst many other more important things, the emergence, perhaps, of a people's Shakespeare.

Notes

1 Stephen Greenblatt, *Renaissance Self-Fashioning,* p. 5.
2 It seems here deeply significant, we may note briefly, that *Measure for Measure* is likely to have been written in the same year as *Othello. Measure for Measure* also explores in some traditional ways, the nature of justice. But Jonathan Dollimore, 'Transgression and Surveillance in *Measure for Measure'* in *Political Shakespeare,* ed. Dollimore and Sinfield, pp. 72—87, points out how that text suggests, too, the way in which power may, to assert its authority and to avoid the more extensive problems which the dominant order itself creates, demonise sexuality. The play also explores aspects of narrative/utterance in the administrative and judicial process. Thus Elbow's view of the meanings of his own language in the court hearing in Act II proves different from that of his audience. Isabella's appeals to Angelo are received by him in ways she never intends. In the final tableau the just appeal made by Isabella to the Duke, before he has made his revelations, poses clearly the problem of how signification may be affected by the situation of the auditors. Power and authority enable the representative of the dominant order to reject an appeal which the audience knows to be entirely just:

> An officer!
> To prison with her! Shall we thus permit
> A blasting and a scandalous breath to fall
> On him so near us?

(V. i. 123; all references to *Measure for Measure* are from *The Riverside Shakespeare,* gen. ed. G. Blakemore Evans, Boston: Houghton Mifflin, 1974.)

To Isabella's earlier proclaimed intentions to reveal Angelo's abuse of power, Angelo himself responds:

> Who will believe thee, Isabel?
> My unsoil'd name, th'austereness of my life,
> My vouch against you, and my place i' th' state,
> Will so your accusation overweigh,
> That you shall stifle in your own report,
> And smell of calumny.
>
> (II. iv. 159)

This recognition of the dangerous opacity of language, the extent to which it may be fashioned and refashioned, either by auditor or by speaker, a recognition moreover that power fully understands this opacity and is ready to exploit it, is contained in *Measure for Measure* by recognition of the apparently crucial difference the presence of the rightful ruler will make to the social order. Thus all the while, the Duke in disguise is present, although his use of trickery to effect justice may itself be said to develop, rather than contain, the play's interrogative thrust.

But in *Othello,* as we observed, in the colonial location, the ruler is absent. The opacity of language, the way in which it may be fashioned to create a response in its auditor, has results that are mostly permitted, untrammelled, fully to effect themselves.

Select Bibliography

Adam, Heribert and Giliomee, Hermann. *The Rise and Crisis of Afrikaner Power.* Cape Town: David Philip, 1979.

Adamson, Jane. *Othello as tragedy: some problems of judgement and feeling.* Cambridge: Cambridge University Press, 1980.

Adler, Doris. 'The Rhetoric of *Black* and *White* in *Othello*', *Shakespeare Quarterly* 25, 1974.

Alexander, Nigel. *Poison, Play and Duel.* London: Routledge and Kegan Paul, 1971.

Ashton, Robert. *The City and the Court 1603–1643.* Cambridge: Cambridge University Press, 1979.

Bald, R.C. '*The Booke of Sir Thomas More* and its Problems', *Shakespeare Survey* 2, 1949.

Baxter, Paul and Sansom, Basil, eds. *Race and Social Difference.* Harmondsworth: Penguin, 1972.

Bevington, David. *Tudor Drama and Politics.* Cambridge, Massachusetts: Harvard University Press, 1968.

Bond, Edward. *Lear.* London: Methuen, 1983.

Bond, Edward. *Bingo.* London: Methuen, 1974.

Bradley, A.C. *Shakespearean Tragedy.* London: Macmillan, 1961.

Bridenbaugh, Carl. *Vexed and Troubled Englishmen 1590–1642.* Oxford: Clarendon Press, 1968.

Brown, J.R. See Shakespeare, William; see Mack, Maynard.

Brown, Paul. ' "This thing of darkness I acknowledge mine": *The Tempest* and the discourse of colonialism' in Jonathan Dollimore and Alan Sinfield eds., *Political Shakespeare.* Manchester: Manchester University Press, 1985.

Butcher, Philip. 'Othello's Racial Identity', *Shakespeare Quarterly* 3, 1952.

Carey, John, ed. *English Renaissance Studies.* Oxford: Clarendon Press, 1980.

Chapman, Michael, ed. *A Century of South African Poetry.* Johannesburg: Ad. Donker, 1985.

Clarke, Cumberland. *Shakespeare and National Character: A study of Shakespeare's knowledge and dramatic and literary use of the distinctive racial characteristics of the different peoples of the world.* London: Hamlin, 1932.

Cooke, Katherine. *A.C. Bradley and his Influence in Twentieth Century Shakespeare Criticism.* Oxford: Oxford University Press, 1972.

Couzens, Tim. 'The Return of the Heart of Darkness', *English Academy Review,* 1982.

Cowhig, Ruth. 'The Importance of Othello's Race', *Journal of Commonwealth Literature* 2, 1977.

Cowhig, Ruth. 'Actors Black and Tawny, in the Role of Othello — and their Critics', *Theatre Research International* 4, 1979.

Cox, Oliver Cromwell. 'Race and Exploitation: A Marxist View' in Paul Baxter and Basil Sansom, eds., *Race and Social Difference.* Harmondsworth: Penguin, 1972.

Danby, John F. *Shakespeare's Doctrine of Nature.* London: Faber and Faber, 1975.

Danson, Lawrence, ed. *On King Lear.* Princeton: Princeton University Press, 1981.

Dean, Leonard F. 'Shakespeare's treatment of conventional ideas', *The Sewanee Review* 52, 1944.

Deitz, Brian. 'England's Overseas Trade in the Reign of James I', in A.G.R. Smith, ed., *The Reign of James VI and I.* London: Macmillan, 1973.

D'Oliveira, John. *Vorster the Man.* Johannesburg: Ernest Stanton Publisher, 1977.

Dollimore, Jonathan. *Radical Tragedy.* Sussex: The Harvester Press, 1984.

Dollimore, Jonathan and Sinfield, Alan. 'History and Ideology: the instance of *Henry V*' in John Drakakis, ed., *Alternative Shakespeares.* London: Methuen, 1985.

Dollimore, Jonathan and Sinfield, Alan, eds. *Political Shakespeare.* Manchester: Manchester University Press, 1985.

Du Toit, André and Giliomee, Hermann. *Afrikaner Political Thought: Analysis and Documents, vol. I 1780—1850.* Cape Town: David Philip, 1983.

Drakakis, John, ed. *Alternative Shakespeares.* London: Methuen, 1985.

Eliot, T.S. *Selected Essays.* London: Faber and Faber, 1958.

Elmes, J.J. 'Some Notes on *Othello*', *Cornhill Magazine* 18, 1868.

Elton, G.R. *Studies in Tudor and Stuart Politics and Government, Papers and Reviews 1946—1972,* vol. II, *Parliament.* Cambridge: Cambridge University Press, 1974.

Elton, G.R. *Studies in Tudor and Stuart Politics and Government, Papers and Reviews 1973—1981,* vol. III. Cambridge: Cambridge University Press, 1983.

Elton, William. *King Lear and the Gods.* California: The Huntington Library, 1966.

Evans, G. Blakemore. See Shakespeare, William.

Evans, K.W. 'The Racial Factor in *Othello'*, *Shakespeare Studies* 5, 1970.

Falk, Doris V. 'Proverbs and the Polonius Destiny', *Shakespeare Quarterly* 4, 1953.

Frye, Roland Mushat. *The Renaissance Hamlet: Issues and Responses in 1600.* Princeton: Princeton University Press, 1984.

Gardner, Helen. 'The Noble Moor', *Proceedings of The British Academy* 41, London: Oxford University Press, 1955.

Giliomee, Hermann. See Du Toit, André; see Adam, Heribert.

Goddard, Harold Clarke. *Alphabet of the Imagination.* New Jersey: Humanities Press, 1974.

Gray, Stephen. 'Plaatje's Shakespeare', *English in Africa* 4:1, 1977.

Greenblatt, Stephen. *Renaissance Self-Fashioning.* Chicago: University of Chicago Press, 1980.

Greenblatt, Stephen, ed. *The Power of Forms in the English Renaissance,* USA: University of Oklahoma, 1982.

Haines, Charles. See Nelson, T.G.A.

Hawkes, Terence, ed. *Coleridge on Shakespeare.* Harmondsworth: Penguin, 1969.

Hawkins, Harriet. 'The Morality of Elizabethan Drama: Some Footnotes to Plato', in John Carey, ed., *English Renaissance Studies.* Oxford: Clarendon Press, 1980.

Heinemann, Margot. *Puritanism and the Theatre.* Cambridge: Cambridge University Press, 1980.

Hill, Christopher. *The Century of Revolution 1603–1714.* Edinburgh: Thomas Nelson, 1962.

Hinman C. See Shakespeare, William.

Hollander, John and Kermode, Frank, eds. *The Literature of Renaissance England.* New York: Oxford University Press, 1973.

Holloway, John. *The Story of the Night.* London: Routledge and Kegan Paul, 1961.

Hope, Christopher. *In the Country of the Black Pig.* Johannesburg: Ravan, 1981.

Horrell, Muriel, ed. *Survey of Race Relations in South Africa 1981.* Johannesburg: South African Institute of Race Relations, 1982.

Hunter, G.K. '*Othello* and Colour Prejudice', *Proceedings of the British Academy* 53, London: Oxford University Press, 1967.

Hurstfield, J. and Sutherland, J., eds. *Shakespeare's World,* London: Edward Arnold, 1964.

Husband, Charles, ed. *'Race' in Britain — Continuity and Change.* London: Hutchinson, 1982.

Jacox, Francis: *Shakespeare Diversions, Second Series: From Dogberry to Hamlet.* 1877.

Jenkins, Harold. See Shakespeare, William.

Johnson, Samuel. 'Proposals for Printing by Subscription The Dramatic Works of William Shakespeare', in Arthur Sherbo, ed., *The Yale Edition of The Works of Samuel Johnson* vol. VII, vol. VIII. New Haven: Yale University Press, 1968.

Jones, Eldred. *The Elizabethan Image of Africa.* Charlottesville: University of Virginia Press, 1971.

Jones, Eldred. *Othello's Countrymen.* London: Oxford University Press, 1965.

Jordan, Winthrop D. *The White Man's Burden: Historical Origins of Racism in the United States.* New York: Oxford University Press, 1974.

Jorgensen, Paul A. *Redeeming Shakespeare's Words.* California: University of California Press, 1962.

Joseph, B.L. *Shakespeare's Eden.* London: Blandford Press, 1971.

Kavanagh, James H. 'Shakespeare in Ideology' in John Drakakis ed., *Alternative Shakespeares.* London: Methuen, 1985.

Kenney, Henry. *Architect of Apartheid.* Johannesburg: Jonathan Ball, 1980.

Kermode, Frank. See Hollander, John.

Kernan, Alvin B. *'King Lear* and the Shakespearean Pageant' in Lawrence Danson, ed., *On King Lear.* Princeton: Princeton University Press, 1981.

Kettle, Arnold. *Shakespeare in a Changing World.* Wellingborough: Lawrence and Wishart, 1964.

Kiernan, V.G. 'European attitudes to the outside world' in Charles Husband, ed., *'Race' in Britain — Continuity and Change.* London: Hutchinson, 1982.

Konrad, George. 'The Long Work of Liberty', *The New York Review of Books,* 26 January 1978.

Kott, Jan. *Shakespeare Our Contemporary.* London: Methuen, 1975.

Lane, Frederick C. *Venice: A Maritime Republic.* Baltimore: Johns Hopkins University Press, 1973.

Leavis, F.R. *The Common Pursuit.* Harmondsworth: Peregrine, 1962.

Lerner, Laurence. 'The Machiavel and the Moor', *Essays in Criticism* 9, 1959.

L'Estrange, Ewen C., ed. *Witch Hunting and Witch Trials. The Indictments for Witchcraft from the Records of 1373 Assizes held for the Home Circuit AD1559—1736.* The London: Kegan Paul, Trench, Trubner and Co., 1929.

190

Lever, J. *The Tragedy of State*. London: Methuen, 1971.

Lever, K. 'Proverbs and *Sententiae* in the Plays of Shakespeare', *The Shakespeare Association Bulletin* 13, 1938.

Levin, Harry. *Shakespeare and the Revolution of the Times*. Oxford: Oxford University Press, 1976.

Lodge, Tom. *Black Politics in South Africa since 1945*. Johannesburg: Ravan, 1983.

Long, Michael. *The Unnatural Scene*. London: Methuen, 1976.

Macey, Samuel L. 'The Naming of the Protagonists in Shakespeare's *Othello*' Notes and Queries 25 : 2, 1978.

Mack, Maynard. 'The Jacobean Shakespeare' in J.R. Brown and B. Harris, eds., *The Jacobean Theatre*. London: Edward Arnold, 1960.

Mack, Maynard. *King Lear in Our Time*. London: Methuen, 1966.

Mahood, Molly. *Shakespeare's Wordplay*. London: Methuen, 1968.

Marovitz, Sanford E. 'Othello Unmasked: A Black Man's Conscience and a White Man's Fool', *Southern Review* 6, 1973.

Matthews, G.M. '*Othello* and the Dignity of Man' in Arnold Kettle, ed., *Shakespeare in a Changing World*. Wellingborough: Lawrence and Wishart, 1964.

Montagu, A. *Man's Most Dangerous Myth*. New York: Oxford University Press, 1974.

Montaigne. *The Essayes of Montaigne,* trans. John Florio, intro. J.I.M. Stewart. USA: Modern Library, no date.

More, Sir Thomas. *Utopia*. London: Everyman, no date.

Muir, Kenneth. 'Shakespeare and Politics' in Arnold Kettle, ed., *Shakespeare in a Changing World*. Wellingborough: Lawrence and Wishart, 1964.

Muir, Kenneth. *Shakespeare's Sources*. London: Methuen, 1965.

Muir, Kenneth. See Shakespeare, William.

Mutloatse, Mothobi, ed. *Forced Landing*. Johannesburg: Ravan, 1980.

Nelson, T.G.A. and Haines, Charles. 'Othello's Unconsummated Marriage', *Essays in Criticism* 33, 1983.

Nkosi, Lewis. *Home and Exile*. USA: Longmans, 1983

Nowottny, Winifred M.T. 'Justice and Love in *Othello*', *University of Toronto Quarterly* 21, 1952.

Nowottny, Winifred M.T. 'Lear's Questions', *Shakespeare Survey* 10, 1957.

Nowottny, Winifred M.T. 'Some Aspects of the Style of *King Lear*', *Shakespeare Survey* 13, 1960.

Nowottny, Winifred M.T. 'Shakespeare's Tragedies' in J. Hurstfield and J. Sutherland, eds., *Shakespeare's World*. London: Edward Arnold, 1964.

O'Meara, Dan. *Volkskapitalisme*. Johannesburg: Ravan, 1983.

Plaatje, Solomon T. 'A South African's Homage' in I. Gollancz, ed., *A Book of Homage to Shakespeare*. London: Oxford University Press, 1916. Reprinted in *English in Africa* 3:2, 1976.

Plaatje, Solomon T. *Native Life in South Africa*. London: P.S. King and Son Ltd., 1916; Johannesburg: Ravan, 1982.

Poisson, Rodney. 'Othello's "Base Indian": A Better Source for the Allusion', *Shakespeare Quarterly* 26, 1975.

Pollard, Alfred W. *et al. Shakespeare's Hand in the Play of Sir Thomas More*. Cambridge: Cambridge University Press, 1923.

Ridley, M.R. See Shakespeare, William.

Rosenthal, E. 'Early Shakespearean Productions in South Africa', *English Studies in Africa* 7:2, 1974.

Shakespeare, William
The First Folio of Shakespeare, ed. C. Hinman. The Norton Facsimile. New York: W.W. Norton and Co., 1968.
The Riverside Shakespeare, ed. G. Blakemore Evans. Boston: Houghton Mifflin, 1974.
Antony and Cleopatra, ed. M.R. Ridley. London: Methuen, 1982.
Hamlet, ed. Harold Jenkins. London: Methuen, 1982.
King Lear, ed. Kenneth Muir. London: Methuen, 1979.
Macbeth, ed. Kenneth Muir. London: Methuen, 1970.
The Merchant of Venice, ed. J.R. Brown. London: Methuen, 1979.
Othello, ed. M.R. Ridley. London: Methuen, 1958.

Sansom, Basil. See Baxter, Paul.

Sepamla, Sipho. *The Root Is One*. London: Rex Collings, 1979.

Shapiro, Barbara J. *Probability and Certainty in Seventeenth Century England*. Princeton: Princeton University Press, 1983.

Sherbo, Arthur, ed. *The Yale Edition of the Works of Samuel Johnson* vol. VII, vol. VIII. New Haven: Yale University Press, 1968.

Simons, H.J. and R.E. *Class and Colour in South Africa 1850–1950*. Harmondsworth: Penguin, 1969.

Sinfield, Alan. *Literature in Protestant England 1560–1660*. London: Croom Helm, 1983.

Sinfield, Alan. See Dollimore, Jonathan. 'History and Ideology: the instance of *Henry V*' in John Drakakis, ed., *Alternative Shakespeares* London: Methuen, 1985.

Sipahigil, T. 'Lewkenor and Othello: an Addendum', *Notes and Queries* 19:4, 1972.

Smith, A.G.R., ed. *The Reign of James VI and I*. London: Macmillan 1973.

Stone, Lawrence. *The Crisis of the Aristocracy 1558—1641*. Oxford: Oxford University Press, 1965.

Stone, Lawrence. *The Causes of the English Revolution 1529—1642*. London: Routledge and Kegan Paul, 1972.

Sutherland, J. See Hurstfield J.

Taylor, Gary. 'Monopolies, Show Trials, Disaster and Invasion: *King Lear* and Censorship' in Gary Taylor and Michael Warren, eds., *The Division of The Kingdoms*. Oxford: Clarendon Press, 1983.

Tennenhouse, Leonard. 'Representing Power: *Measure for Measure* in Its Time' in Stephen Greenblatt, ed., *The Power of Forms in the English Renaissance*. USA: University of Oklahoma, 1982.

Tillyard, E.M.W. *The Elizabethan World Picture*. London: Chatto & Windus, 1967.

Tomaselli K.G. See Visser, Nick.

Van Onselen, Charles. *Studies in the Social and Economic History of the Witwatersrand 1886—1914:2*. Johannesburg: Ravan, 1982.

Van Wyk, Christopher. *It is Time to Go Home*. Johannesburg: Ad. Donker, 1979.

Vickers, Brian, ed. *Shakespeare, The Critical Heritage*, 2. London: Routledge and Kegan Paul, 1974.

Visser, Nick and Tomaselli, K.G., eds., *Critical Arts: A Journal for Media Studies* 3:2. Universities of Rhodes and Witwatersrand, 1984.

Wallerstein, Immanuel. *The Capitalist World-Economy*. Cambridge: Cambridge University Press, 1979.

Wallerstein, Immanuel. *The Modern World-System: Capitalist Agriculture and The Origins of the European World-Economy in the Sixteenth Century*. New York: Academic Press, 1974.

Warren, Michael. See Taylor, Gary.

Weimann, Robert. 'The Soul of the Age: Towards A Historical Approach to Shakespeare' in Arnold Kettle, ed., *Shakespeare in a Changing World*. Wellingborough: Lawrence and Wishart, 1964.

Wright, Louis B. 'Colonial Developments in the Reign of James I' in A.G.R. Smith, ed., *The Reign of James VI and I*. London: Macmillan, 1973.

Wrightson, Keith. *English Society 1580—1660*. London: Hutchinson, 1982.

Index

Hurstfield, J. 55 n3 & 7
Husband, Charles 104, 117 n6
Hutchings, Geoffrey 103, 125
 n74

Isle of Dogs, The 148
Isle of Gulls, The 144, 148

Jacox, Francis 126 n83
James I 27, 30, 71, 90, 140,
 142—50, 163, 176 n40 & 41,
 183
Jenkins, Harold 55 n1, 58 n40
Jenkinson, Antony 89, 123 n54
Johnson, Samuel 13, 21 n2, 130,
 147
Jones, Eldred 60, 62, 113, 117
 n4 & 8, 125 n63
Jonson, Ben 62, 144, 148
Jordan Winthrop 60—1, 66, 68,
 91, 117 n5
Jorgensen, Paul A. 81, 120 n39
 & 40
Joseph, B.L. 25—6, 55 n3
Julius Caesar 170

Kavanagh, James H. 54, 58 n42,
 168—9
Kenney, Henry 56 n21
Kermode, Frank 129 n102
Kernan, Alvin B. 173 n16
Kettle, Arnold 21 n8, 22 n14
Kiernan, V.G. 60, 117 n6
King Lear 14, 20, 26, 96,
 130—72, 184
Konrad, George 37, 56 n24
Knack to Know an Honest Man,
 A 81
Knack to Know a Knave, A 81,
 120 n40

Kott, Jan 26, 55 n4
Kunene, Mazisi 156, 177 n50

Lane, Frederic C. 121 n51
Leavis, F.R. 79, 100, 105—6,
 110, 126 n 79
Levin, Harry 130, 172 n2
Leo, John 62
Lerner, Laurence 100, 108—9,
 110, 127 n86
Lever, J.W. 143, 144
Lever, K. 56 n19
Lewkenor, Sir Lewis 119 n27
Lodge, Tom 173 n10
Lok, John 118 n13
Long, Michael 46—7, 57 n36
Lust's Dominion 62

Macbeth 81—2, 184
Macey, Samuel L. 129 n90
Machiavelli, Niccolo 132
Mack, Maynard 149, 177 n47
Mahood, Molly 56 n20
Marovitz, Sanford E. 127 n84
Marston, John 148
Martyr, Peter 98
Mary I 29—30
Mary, Queen of Scots 30
'Masque of Blackness' 62
Mattera, Don 167, 180 n60
Matthews, G.M. 119 n22
Measure for Measure 96, 149—50,
 169, 185 n2
Merchant of Venice, The 72—3,
 78—9
Montagu, Ashley 112, 128 n94
Montaigne, Michel 113—4, 129
 n101
More, Sir Thomas 167, 180 n59
Muir, Kenneth 16, 21 n8, 55 n3,
 119 n26, 121 n42
Mustapha 144
Mutloatse, Mothobi 17, 22 n12